Start Powerboating

机动艇起步

[英]乔恩·门德斯　著
王超　译

Illustrations by Pete Galvin
Technical Editor Paul Mara
First Published 2006

The Royal Yachting Association, RYA House, Ensign Way, Hamble, Southampton, SO31 4YA
www.rya.org.uk
Cover design: Pete Galvin
Photographic credits: McMurdo, Piplers of Poole, Garmin, Icom, RNLI, Jon Mendez, PPL, Paul Mara, Laurence West, Seaward Marine, Bisham Abbey School of Navigation, Scorpion RIBs, Paul Glatzel and Musto.

哈尔滨工程大学出版社
Harbin Engineering University Press

黑版贸审字 08-2020-068

内容简介

本书主要介绍了英国皇家游艇协会机动艇驾驶的基本操作技术要领、驾驶机动艇前的准备要求及驾驶机动艇时遇到危险情况的应急处理方法等。

本书适合帆船爱好者及帆船培训机构使用。

图书在版编目（CIP）数据

机动艇起步 /（英）乔恩•门德斯著；王超译. -- 哈尔滨：哈尔滨工程大学出版社，2020.4

ISBN 978-7-5661-2606-1

Ⅰ. ①机… Ⅱ. ①乔… ②王… Ⅲ. ①机动船—航海运动—运动训练 Ⅳ. ①G874

中国版本图书馆 CIP 数据核字（2020）第 054068 号

选题策划 史大伟 薛 力
责任编辑 唐欢欢
封面设计 李海波

出版发行 哈尔滨工程大学出版社
社　　址 哈尔滨市南岗区南通大街 145 号
邮政编码 150001
发行电话 0451-82519328
传　　真 0451-82519699
经　　销 新华书店
印　　刷 武汉精一佳印刷有限公司
开　　本 787 mm×1 092 mm 1/16
印　　张 3.5
字　　数 106 千字
版　　次 2020 年 4 月第 1 版
印　　次 2020 年 4 月第 1 次印刷
定　　价 89.00 元
http://www.hrbeupress.com
E-mail：heupress@hrbeu.edu.cn

Sustainable Forests

EMAS
VERIFIED ENVIRONMENTAL MANAGEMENT

Contents 目录

How to Start Powerboating
如何开始从事机动艇活动

For many people the chance to go out on the water and try a boat starts with a trip on a friend's boat, most first time powerboaters come back hooked and want more! A RYA Powerboat training course allows you the best of both worlds – your chance to drive someone else's boat and the opportunity to gain the experience and knowledge to be safe afloat. More importantly you will come away understanding how boats work, the equipment you will need and the type, style and design features that you would want on your boat should you decide to purchase one.
对很多人来说，第一次出海玩船往往是受邀登上朋友的船只，而绝大多数机动艇玩家第一次体验回来后都上瘾了，欲罢不能！RYA机动艇培训课程能够为你带来两方面的好处：让你驾驶别人的船，以及能够让你获得驾驶经验和相关知识以确保水上安全。更为重要的是，你将了解到船只如何运转，你需要的设备和类型，你想要购买的船只的风格和设计特点。

If you are lucky enough to already own a boat the knowledge you gain will enable you to use your boat safely, to handle it more confidently and to really enjoy the sport.
如果你拥有一条船，该课程提供的知识可以帮助你安全地驾船、自信地操作，以及充分地享受这项运动。

This book is designed to accompany the RYA Powerboat courses:
本书配合如下RYA机动艇课程：
Level 1 Introduction to Powerboating
级别一，机动艇介绍
Level 2 Powerboat Handling
级别二，机动艇操纵
Level 2 is the recognised minimum standard for powerboat skippers
级别二是机动艇船长的最低认证标准

If you hold Level 2, Powerboat Handing and are a British passport holder or British resident you are eligible for an International Certificate of Competence for power craft up to 10m in length.
如果你持有级别二资格证书，即机动艇操纵，并持有英国护照或者英国居留证，那么就有资格获得国际10 m以下机动艇驾驶合规证书。

Personal Buoyancy and Clothing
个人助浮衣以及着装

Before you consider going afloat you need to make a list of personal equipment you will use. The most important item will be your choice of either lifejackets or buoyancy aids for yourself and your crew.
在考虑下水之前，你需要列出你所需的装备清单，其中最重要的是你自己以及你的船员的救生衣或助浮衣。

Lifejackets are designed to turn an unconscious casualty in the water face up. Most are powered by a small gas canister which can be activated automatically when it comes in contact with the water. Automatic ones are especially good for children and those who are not confident in the water.
救生衣可以帮助失去意识的落水者在水中保持脸朝上。救生衣大多的设计是人员落水后其靠气瓶自动启动充气。自动充气救生衣对儿童或者在水中缺乏自信的人特别有效。

A buoyancy aid provides some buoyancy but not as much as a lifejacket and will not turn an unconscious person face up. However it will support a conscious swimmer. They are ideal for sports where you get very wet, are a good swimmer and are confident in the water. An automatic lifejacket is the best option if you are alone on a boat.
Wear a lifejacket or buoyancy aid unless you are sure you don't need to.
助浮衣能够提供一定的浮力但其没有救生衣浮力大，而且无法帮助失去意识的人员把脸转向朝上。但是，它可以帮助有意识的游泳者。这对于经常下水的运动者、游泳好手并且在水中有自信的人是理想的装备。如果你单独驾艇，自动救生衣是最好的选择。
建议你穿戴救生衣或者助浮衣，除非你确认绝不需要它。

Outer clothing 其他服装

There is a vast array of clothing available to suit all budgets and weather conditions, here are some examples.
针对不同的预算和天气条件，有如下一系列类型的服装可供选择。

Hot weather 炎热气候

Even when it is very hot you will need a minimum of a top, shorts, suitable footwear and don't forget a hat and plenty of sun cream. Remember to take a wind/waterproof jacket; when the sun goes in it soon gets very chilly.

即使是非常炎热的天气，你也至少需要穿着上衣、短裤以及合适的鞋子并且不要忘记戴帽子和带足够的防晒霜。记得带一件防风、防水夹克，因为太阳落山后可能马上就会降温。

Cool weather 凉爽天气

More substantial windproof and waterproof clothing and boots are required, preferably with breathable under-layers.
穿更厚一些的防风、防水衣和靴子，最好都是带有透气内层的。

Cold and extreme weather 寒冷和极端天气

When out on the water in cold weather or for long periods it is well worth the investment in buying a dry suit. Fitted with special seals to keep the water out they can be worn over normal clothing or breathable layers. Excellent also if you are a safety boat crew because they allow you to enter the water and stay dry. Some people who expect to get wet prefer a wetsuit.
如果在寒冷天气下水或者长时间在水中时，你应该购买一件干式保暖服。这种衣服配有特制的封条以防止水流进去，这样在里面就可以穿着保暖和透气的常规服装。这种服装也是救生艇船员的理想装备，因为其可以使你下水救人后还能保持身体干燥。当然有些下水的人更倾向于湿式保暖服。

Other items to consider taking are hats, sunglasses, sun cream, goggles, drinks, water, snack foods, medication (including anti-seasickness pills or bands) and a towel.
其他要携带的装备包括帽子、太阳镜、防晒霜、护目镜、饮料、水、零食、药品（晕船药或者晕船贴）和毛巾。

Parts of the Boat
船上部件

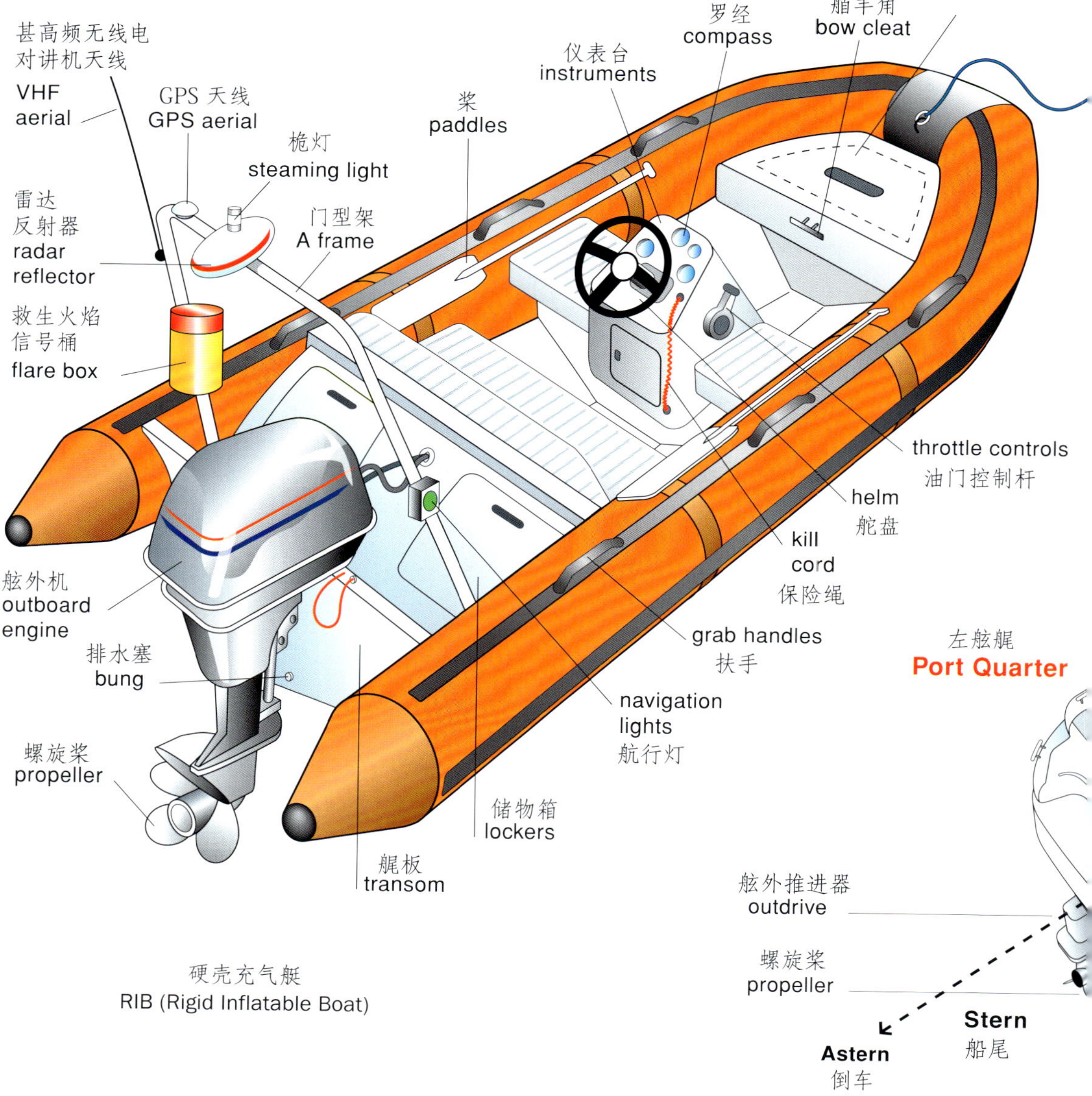

硬壳充气艇
RIB (Rigid Inflatable Boat)

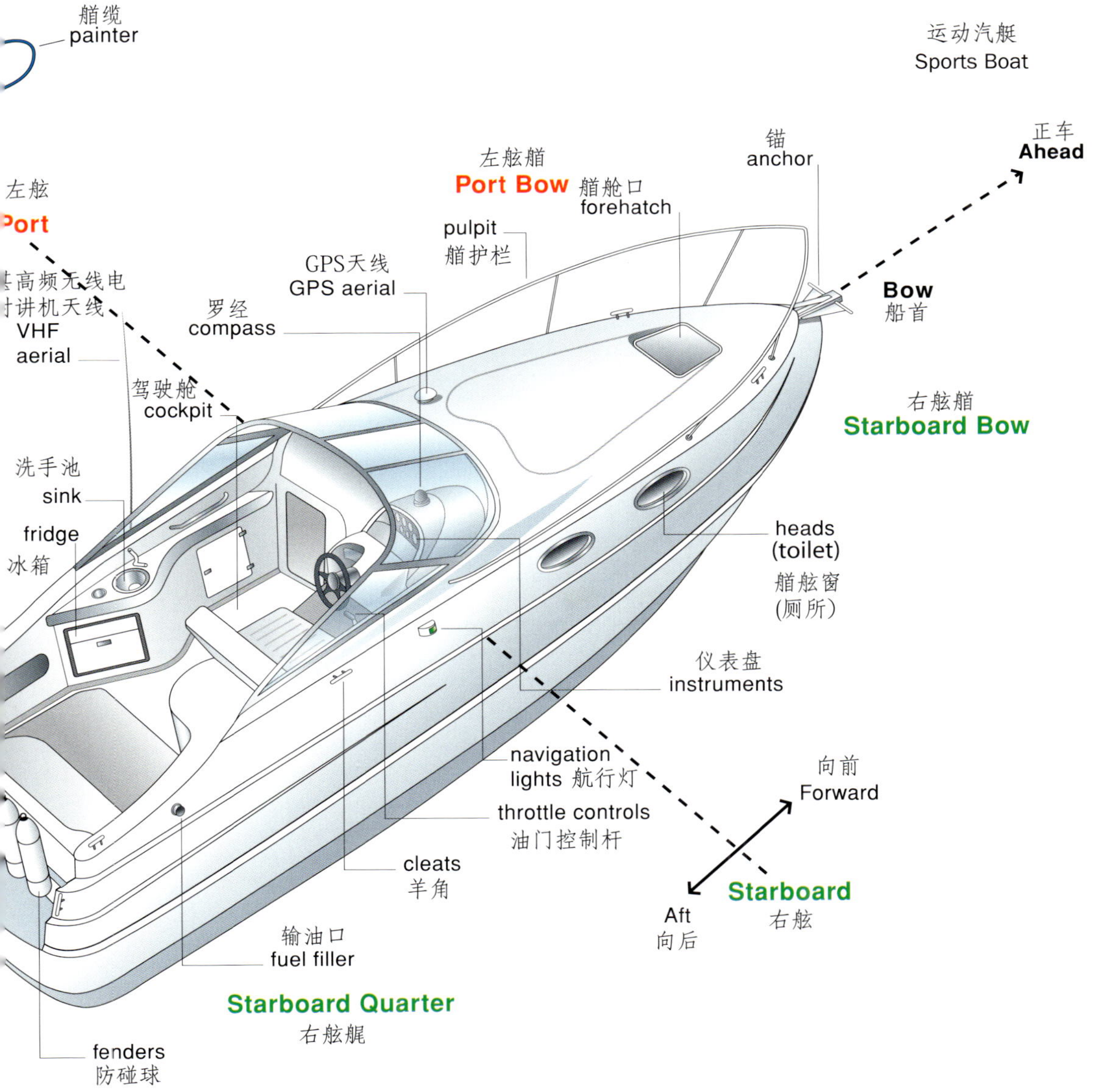

艏缆
painter
运动汽艇
Sports Boat
正车
Ahead
锚
anchor
左舷艏
Port Bow
艏舱口
forehatch
左舷
Port
pulpit
艏护栏
GPS天线
GPS aerial
高频无线电
讲机天线
VHF
aerial
罗经
compass
Bow
船首
驾驶舱
cockpit
右舷艏
Starboard Bow
洗手池
sink
fridge
冰箱
heads
(toilet)
艏舷窗
(厕所)
仪表盘
instruments
navigation
lights 航行灯
向前
Forward
throttle controls
油门控制杆
cleats
羊角
Starboard
右舷
Aft
向后
输油口
fuel filler
Starboard Quarter
右舷艉
fenders
防碰球

Types of Craft 船只类型

There are many different types and sizes of small powered boats available, below is a selection of the most popular.
小型机动艇有多种类型、多种尺寸，以下章节简述最为常见的。

RIB (Rigid Inflatable Boat) 硬壳充气艇

Vee hull with inflatable tubes for buoyancy and stability. Tubes also cushion the ride when it is rough, however this creates less internal volume as tubes take up space.
Good rescue boat but now also popular as a family and fishing boat. A well-designed and driven RIB can handle seas far in excess of those handled by other comparable sized boats. Usually fitted with outboard engines, some larger boats are fitted with inboard engines.
V形艇体配有充气胎以增加浮力和稳性。充气胎可以在严酷天气航行时起到缓冲垫的作用，但因为充气胎占用一定空间，所以这种艇内部空间较小。
其非常适合作为救援船使用，现在也常作为家庭艇或钓鱼艇。设计卓越并由技术高超驾驶员驾驶的硬壳充气艇远远强于绝大多数同尺寸的船只，其能应付各种海况。大多数船只配备舷外机，有些大型的配有舷内机。

Sports Boat 运动汽艇

Good all round family craft in flat to slight seas. Better internal volume than a RIB, but ultimately poorer sea keeping and usually drier. Available with outboard or inboard engines. Many people start their boating with this style of boat.
其是全面而良好的家庭用船，适于在平静和轻浪海况上航行。其比硬壳充气艇有更为优化的内部空间，但是其耐波性较差，也更干燥。其可配舷外机或舷内机。很多人是通过接触这种船才开始玩船的。

Both RIBs and Sportsboats have a planing hull, this can be shallow or deep Vee. Shallow Vees plane easily and give a flatter wake but slam more in poor sea conditions. Flatter panels aft allow the hull to skim across the surface. A Deep Vee gives a smooth ride in rougher water but requires more power to propel it.

以上两种船都是滑行型船体，浅V或深V形船中，浅V形很容易滑行而且只产生平缓的尾波，但是在恶劣海况下更容易使船体撞浪从而产生不舒适感。艉部更平的船底可以让船体滑过水面。深V形船只在恶劣海况下驾驶更平稳，但其需要更强的动力。

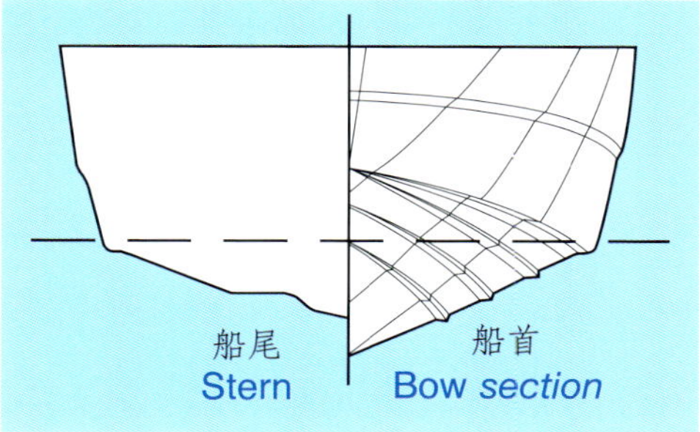

Displacement Hull 排水型船体

The classic fishing hull and more rounded (duck shape). Works by pushing water out of the way as they move. Good sea boats but are slow and inclined to roll.

传统渔船船体和拥有更圆（鸭身型）的线型的船，它们前进时把水推开。其是拥有良好耐波性的航海船只，但是速度慢而且很容易造成横摇。

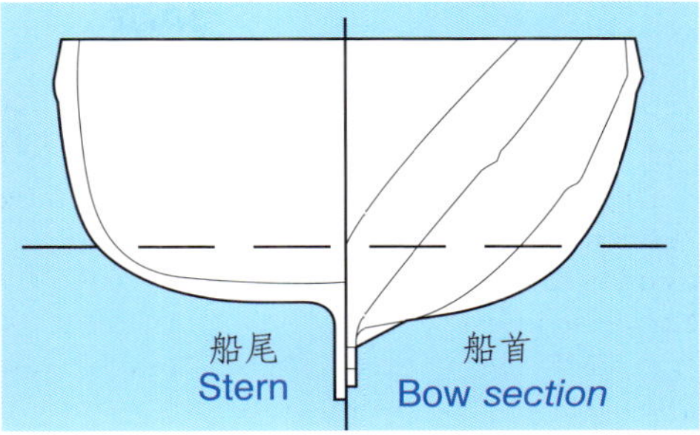

Semi-Displacement Hull 半排水型船体

Combines some of the features of both the displacement and the Vee hull. Good sea keeping with moderate speed. Needs a lot of power to go fast, so can use a lot of fuel.

其兼顾了排水型和V形船的一些特点。其拥有低速、良好的耐波性的特点。其需要很大动力才能快速行驶，因此耗油很大。

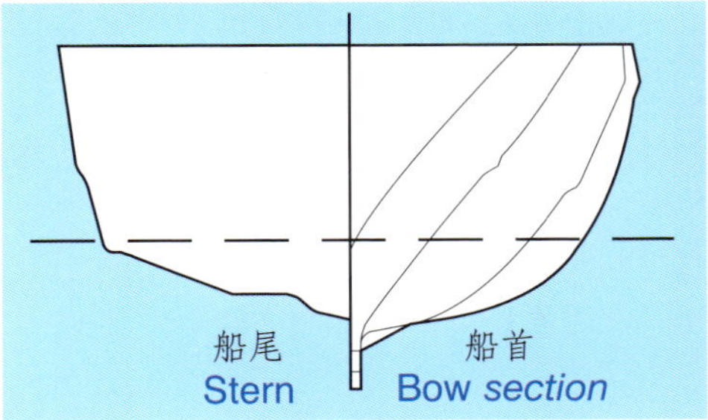

Dory or Cathedral Hull 小型平底船或大教堂型（多壳）船体

Stable with an open deck, good load carrying capacity, low power will make it plane.
Hard ride in choppy water.

其稳定性良好，拥有开放甲板、大载重，不需要较大的动力就能滑行，但其在激浪海面上很难驾驶。

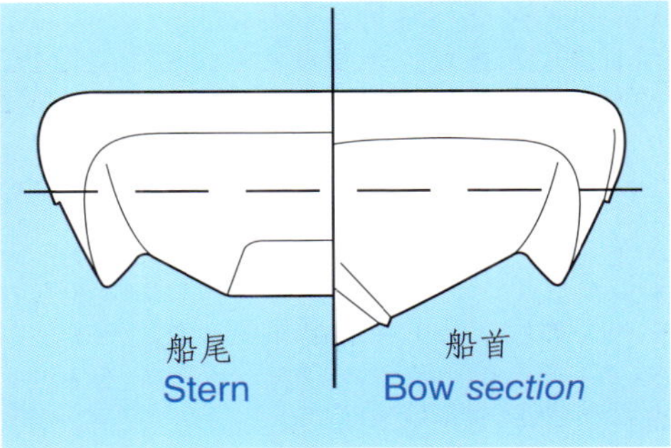

Engines and Drives 发动机和驱动方式

Small boats are powered by several different types of engine and drive systems. For small planing craft the outboard is still the most popular engine especially since the newest outboards are so much quieter, lighter and economical. The propeller is still the most popular way to transmit engine power to the water.

有几种发动机和推进器系统可以装配到小型船只上。小型滑行艇常配舷外机，尤其是现在的最新型的舷外机更安静、更轻便和更节约燃油。螺旋桨仍然是最为常用的动力传输推进方式。

Drive types 推进类型

Inboard engine with shaft drive 舷内机配传动轴驱动

Engine is within the hull and drives a gearbox and shaft. The shaft passes through the hull on a fitting called a stern gland making a watertight seal. Steering is achieved with a rudder. A simple system that is reliable and generally low maintenance.

发动机装在船舱内，通过变速箱和传动轴驱动。传动轴通过水密的装置穿过船体，这个装置叫作艉轴管压盖。其通过舵来实现转向。这是一种常见而可靠的系统，维护费用低。

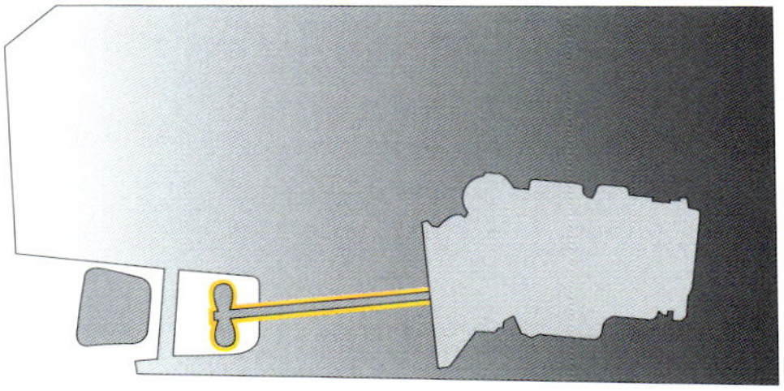

An Outdrive or Stern drive 舷外驱动或艉驱动

Engine is within the hull but this time it drives an outdrive on the back of the hull. While steering the unit pivots from side to side and can be tilted enabling it to travel through shallow water. However this system means that there are lots of mechanical parts in the water all the time.
发动机装在船舱内，但发动机驱动装在船舷外。操舵转向的时候，舷外推动机可以左右转向，而且可以调整纵倾角度以便在浅水中行驶。但是这种系统意味着大量的机械部件都置于水中。

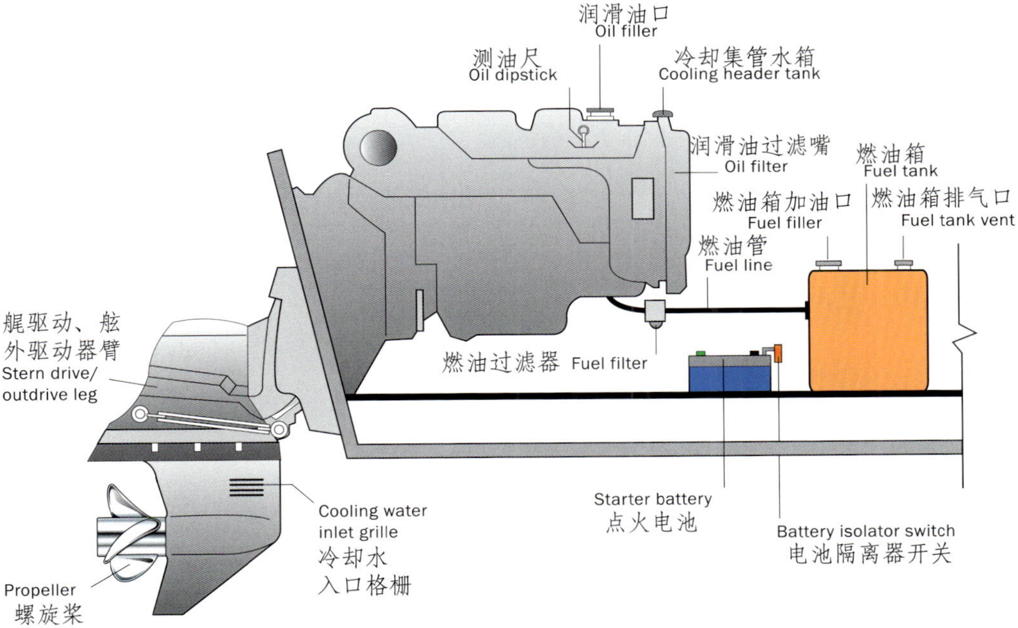
润滑油口
Oil filler
测油尺
Oil dipstick
冷却集管水箱
Cooling header tank
润滑油过滤嘴
Oil filter
燃油箱
Fuel tank
燃油箱加油口
Fuel filler
燃油箱排气口
Fuel tank vent
燃油管
Fuel line
艉驱动、舷外驱动器臂
Stern drive/
outdrive leg
燃油过滤器 Fuel filter
Cooling water
inlet grille
冷却水
入口格栅
Starter battery
点火电池
Battery isolator switch
电池隔离器开关
Propeller
螺旋桨

Outboard 舷外机

Whole engine and drive train are carried on the stern of the boat. A self-contained unit that pivots and tilts just like an outdrive, but has the benefit that the drive can be tilted clear of the water when not in use. Smaller ones are tiller steered and can be stolen. Larger ones usually have wheel steering and a seated driving position.

舷外机即整个发送机和驱动装置都装在船尾舷外。其拥有独立的单元，能够像舷外驱动系统一样绕轴转动或者能够纵倾，而且在不使用的时候，驱动装置能够调整纵倾到水面以上。更小的舷外机通过舵柄操控方向，但有被盗的风险。大型舷外机通过舵轮操作，并配有驾驶员座位。

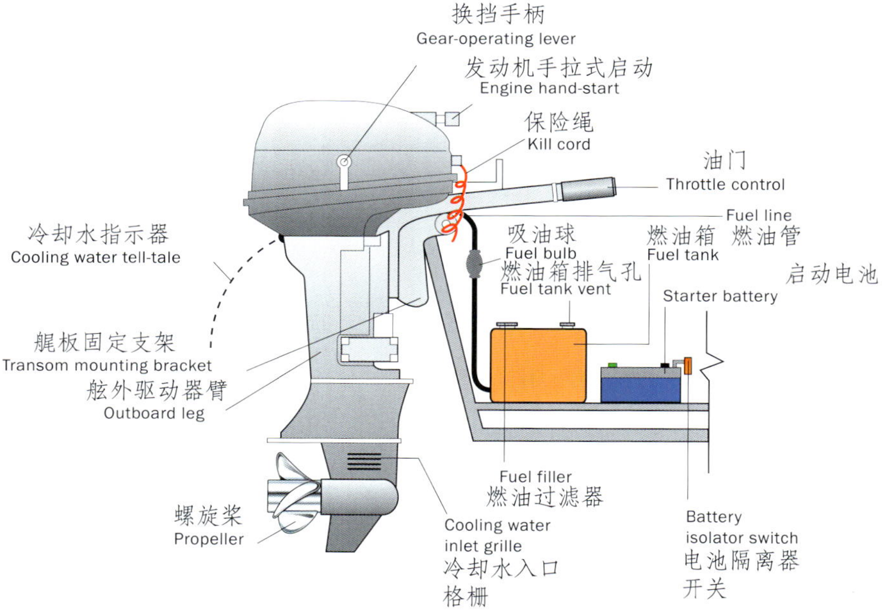

Jet drive 喷射式推进器

High volume pump (impellor) sucks water from under the boat. It is squirted out of a movable nozzle at the stern. This provides steering and with the aid of a clam cover, reverse gear. They are great for shallow water but can lose power in rougher weather due to the pump inlet lifting out of the water.

大容量泵（叶轮机）从船下方吸水，水通过可转向的喷嘴喷射出去。转向喷嘴具有操舵转向功能，而且借助齿轮能够倒挡。其非常适合浅水区，但在恶劣天气情况下，由于泵的吸水口提升到水面，可能会失去动力。

Boat Controls
船只控制

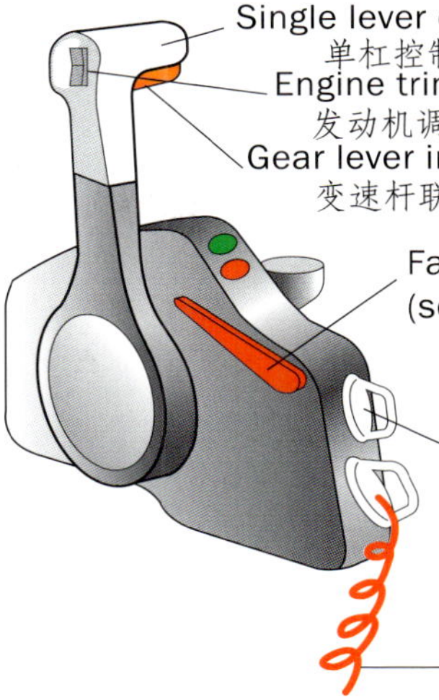

Most powerboats have a single lever control with neutral in the centre, pushing the lever forward engages ahead gear, pulling it backwards gives astern gear. Pushing the lever further in either direction increases the revolutions and hence the speed. Many tiller steered craft have a twist grip throttle on the tiller arm and a separate gear lever on the side of the engine, the latest have a combined gear / throttle on the hand grip. The trim control is used to raise and lower the leg. It also allows the drive angle to be optimised for sea conditions and loading.

大多数船都配有单操纵杆，其中间位置为空挡，向前推控制杆调到前进挡，往后拉是倒挡。向任意方向继续推杆会提高转速，即加速。很多舵杆型的船在舵杆上还装有一个油门转钮和在发动机上装有一个独立的挡位杆。最新型设计的船把挡位和油门合并在一个手柄上。纵倾控制杆可以抬起或者放下支架，也可控制推进角度以便在不同海况和装载条件下优化操作。

Kill cord **保险绳**

The Kill cord is very important. It's there for everyone's safety. Its purpose is to stop the engine if you move away from the helm, or fall out. It also stops the boat running away and injuring you or others. Always check that the kill cord works. Attach it to yourself preferably around the leg, EVERY time that you go boating.

保险绳非常重要，这是为了保证所有人的安全。其作用是，如果你离开操舵位置或者落水，它将自动关机。它也能同时防止船只自已开走撞伤你或其他人。确保保险绳总是有效的。每次登船时都要把它绑在腿上！

Before Starting **启动前**

Check that it is not in gear, the propeller is clear, start whilst in neutral. Some engines need either choke or extra revs to start. When it starts, check the cooling water is exiting. Use the gear lever interlock correctly, you need to squeeze it to engage gear. Release after each engagement of gears. Always allow a pause in neutral when moving from ahead to astern gear. Use a solid push to put the craft into gear – without dragging of the gears. Check that the steering operates smoothly from lock to lock and without the need for excessive effort. Turn the wheel in the direction you wish the boat to move. Always steer before engaging gear. It is best practice to use one hand for the steering and one for the gears (throttle), this is especially important at higher speed. Tiller steered boats require you to push or pull the tiller in the opposite direction to the direction you want to go.

检查确定在空挡，螺旋桨附近无障碍物，空挡时开机。有些发动机需要风门或拉线转动才能启动。启动后，检查冷却水流出。正确地使用挡位锁，需要按压才能上挡。到挡位后松开按锁。在每次正车换倒车挡的时候，要在空挡停顿一下。用力推挡杆使船进入挡位，而不是在挡位间慢慢拖带。检查是否可以顺畅操舵，不费力地能从一侧满舵打到另一侧满舵。调舵盘到你想要的方向。上挡加油前必须先调好舵位。最佳的操作方法是一手控舵一手控舵杆（油门），在高速行驶时这一点尤其重要。操控配备舵杆的船只，你要拉舵或推舵朝向转向的相反方向。

Operating at Planing Speed 高速滑行时的操控

When intending to travel at higher speeds, you must keep a really good all round look-out. Check it is clear before you turn, be aware of other water users and the effect of your wash. Load and trim the boat according to the conditions and don't go boating when it is beyond your or your boat's abilities. Operators of craft wih more powerful engines should make themselves aware of the handling characteristics of these craft and consider undertaking training appropriate to these boats. The RYA Intermediate and Advanced courses will prepare you for faster and more powerful craft. Ensure all crew are appropriately seated with secure handholds before setting off. When operating at speed, be aware that the motion in the forward end of the boat will be more noticealble than it will be further aft. In general, and subject to the boat being trimmed appropriately, passengers will have a safer and more comfortable ride when seated aft rather than forward.

当需要高速行驶时，你必须时刻保持非常好的全局瞭望。根据海况装载船只、调整纵倾，如果天气条件超过你或者你的船只的能力范围，不要出海。船只操作者在使用马力强劲的引擎时应知道这些船只的操作特点并考虑参加相关的培训。RYA中级和高级课程为你提供操作更大马力和更高速度的船只的培训。在出发前确保所有船员都已坐好，并有安全的扶手。当在高速行驶时，要注意船前端的情况比船尾端更容易被观察到。一般来说，在确保船只平衡的情况下，乘客在船的后部比在前端更舒适和安全。

Crew and Rope Work 船员和结绳技术

Your crew are your best asset on the boat, with a well trained crew your boating will be far safer and enjoyable. Teach them to throw a line, tie a few simple knots and how to cleat off.
你的船员是你船上最重要的。有一个训练有素的船员团队能使你驾船更安全和有趣。教会他们如何抛绳、打绳结和在羊角上系缆、解缆。

Round Turn and Two Half Hitches—Easy to tie and can be undone whilst under load.
木结：很容易打的绳结，而且其能够在受力状态下方便地解开。

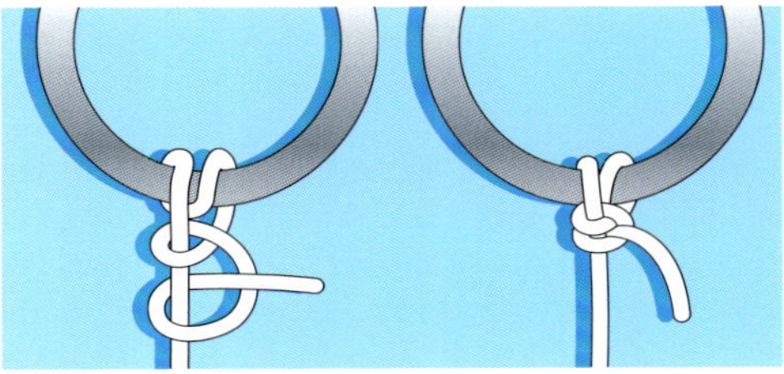

Clove Hitch - Good for fenders and light loads, can work loose.
双套结：适用于系防碰球和承担小载荷，但容易松动。

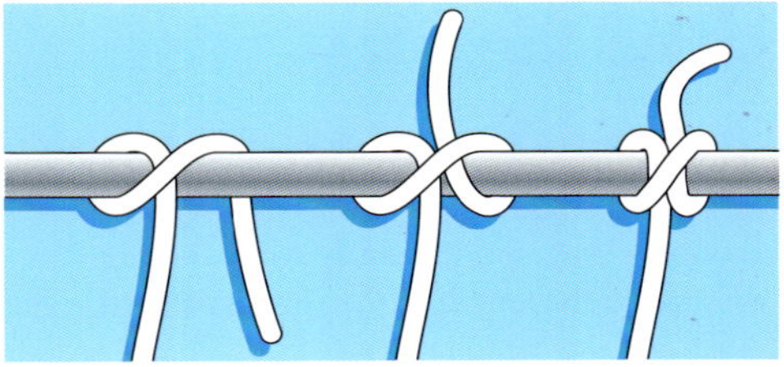

Sheet Bend—Good for joining two lines, especially if they are different diameters. Can only be undone without a load on.
单编结：非常适合连接两根绳子，尤其是直径不同的绳子。其只能在不受力状态下解开。

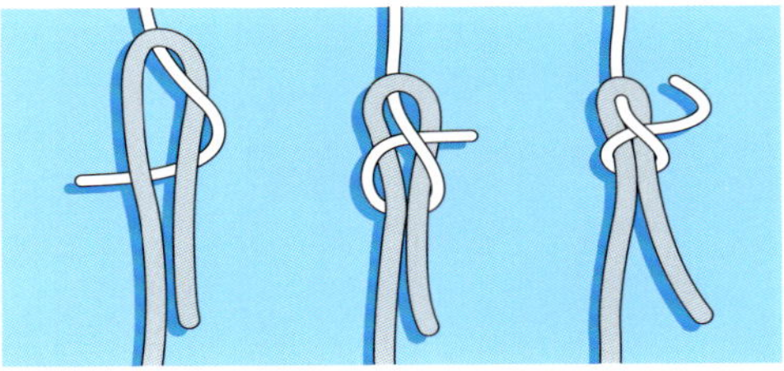

Cleating Off—Take a complete turn around the cleat, then follow this with two figures of eight, finish with a complete turn.
羊角结：在羊角上绕一圈，然后接着绕两个8字，最后以一个圈结束。

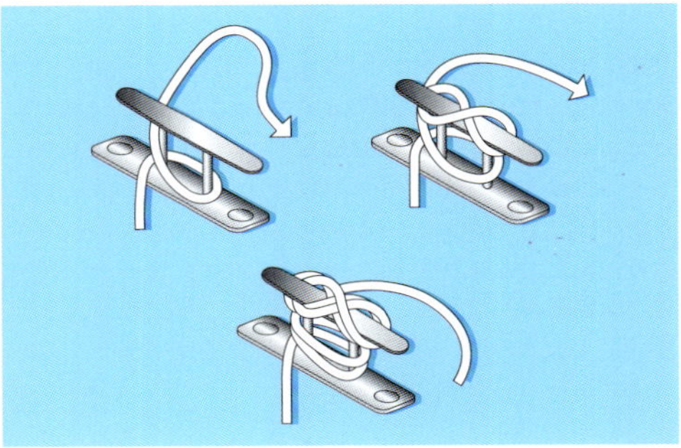

Bowline—The most used knot in boating, good for mooring lines. Will take a great load and can still be released. Can only be undone when there is no load.
单套结：船上最常用的绳结，可用于系泊缆绳。其在承受很大的力后也可以解开，但需要在不受力状态下解开。

Trailing and Launching 用拖车拖带和下水

Trailing your boat allows you to explore many other boating areas. It can also reduce your boating costs, because you do not have to pay marina fees, although some harbour authorities do charge to launch a boat. The laws on trailing can be complicated: check with the RYA (www.rya.org.uk) or your national Highways Agency websites for full details. Practise driving a car with a trailer; remember that the whole unit is much larger than just a car and will require extra room to manoeuvre. Allow more time when you need to brake.
开拖车拖带船只能够让你发现更多玩船的水域。其也可以减少一些费用，因为这样就不用支付码头费用，但有些码头管理处还是会征收一定的下水费。与拖带有关的法律很复杂，查询RYA网站(www.rya.org.uk)或你所在国家相关部门的网站可获得更为详细的信息。练习拖车拖带驾驶，注意，（帆船）加上拖车后的长度比汽车本身会长很多，因此你需要更多的操作空间。刹车的时候也需要预留更多时间。

On arrival at your launch site you need to allow the wheel bearings on the trailer to cool before you launch, cold sea water can seep past the bearing seals and cause corrosion. Whilst waiting you can assess the launch area and slipway, noting how steep it is and any obstructions or other hazards. Be aware as to the length of the slipway and how it ends. You will also need to find secure parking for the trailer and tow vehicle. Many of the items, which need to be considered for launching, can be prepared beforehand, e.g. weather forecasts, tidal information, ownership of the slipway, permission to launch or harbour dues.
抵达下水点后，你需要先让拖车轮毂轴承落下来，冷海水可能会渗透进入轴承而造成腐蚀。等待下水的时候，你可以分析船台和下水区域，评估斜度，检查是否有障碍物，了解船台的长度和它的终点的状况。你还需要确认拖车和汽车的停车位。大多下水前需要考虑的事项，都要事先准备好，比如天气预报、潮流信息、船台的所有权，以及下水许可或码头费用等。

Pre Launch checks 下水前的检查

Remove trailer board straps and cover, insert bung and check the boat, engine and propeller for damage, load the boat with equipment and supplies. If running water is available you can start and pre warm the engine using the muffs.
拆掉绑扎带和盖布，插入塞子，检查船、螺旋桨、发动机，装载船上的设备和补给。如果有供水，开机预热。

Launching 下水

Aim to float the boat off the trailer; you may need a long rope or a bar to keep the tow vehicle out of the water. When it is afloat release the winch strap and push the boat off or start the engine with it partially raised and reverse it clear. Now either get your crew to hold the boat in the deeper water or move it to a pontoon making sure that the tow vehicle and trailer are parked well clear of the slipway.

为使船从拖车上浮起来，你可能需要足够长的绳子或者连杆以免拖车掉进水里。当船浮起来后，松掉绑带，把船推开或在发动机抬起一半的状态下启动发动机并倒船离开。然后可以请你的船员把船拽到深水里，也可以移船到泊位，然后带着拖车开车离开下水点并停好。

Recovery **回收船只上岸**

This is a reversal of the launch process; however it is essential that nobody gets between the boat and the shore (especially if on a lee shore) or trailer. Remember to raise the engine on the approach but keep the cooling water circulating. Unwind the winch strap keeping hands clear of the winch handle. Attach the winch strap and ideally a second line before you pull it clear of the water. Flush the engine through at the earliest opportunity.

回收船只上岸是上面步骤的相反过程。一定要注意，人不能停留在船和岸或拖车之间（尤其是迎风岸）。注意，靠近的时候要抬高发动机但是要保持冷却水循环工作。解开绞车带，注意手要避开绞车手柄。绑上绞车带，在船只拉出水面之前最好绑上第二根绳子。尽快用清水冲洗发动机。

Before towing **用拖车拖带之前**

Ensure the boat is fully secure on the trailer. Use tie-down straps on the D-rings on the transom to hold the rear of the boat to the trailer. Connect the D-ring on the bow to hold the front of the boat in position. Use a safety chain between the vehicle and the trailer in case the two become separated. Re-attach the trailer board, check that the lights work and off you go.

确保船只完全固定在拖车上。用绑扎带绑住艉板的D环，以便在拖车上固定船的尾部。连接船首D环确保船首到位。加一条安全链连接汽车和拖车，以防二者分离。重新固定拖车架到汽车拖钩上。检查艉灯是否运行良好。

Boat Handling 操船

Some points to consider when handling a boat: How much windage it has, how the stream affects it, how much momentum it has, is there any prop effect, where does it pivot and how is it steered?
操船需要考虑的一些因素：多大的对风面风阻，流会怎样影响船只，船有多大动力，是否有螺旋桨转艏效应，转向轴心在哪里和如何操舵等？

The natural elements 自然因素

Windage 对风面

Vessel A has much greater areas exposed to the wind than B—this means that its windage is higher; this must be taken into account when handling the boat especially in a marina environment.
船A比船B具有更大的受风面积，也就是对风面更大，风阻更大。尤其是在码头环境开船时，必须考虑到这一点。

Stream 流

Stream like windage affects all craft in different ways, a displacement craft (B) with a keel will be more affected by stream than windage, but the high sided small cruiser (A) with a planing hull will be more affected by wind than stream.
和风一样，流对不同的船有不同的影响，对于带龙骨的排水型船（B），流的影响大于风的影响，但是对于滑水型船体的高干舷高速小游艇（A），风的影响大于流的影响。

A

B

Your boat's characteristics 船的特征

Momentum—Carrying way & stopping 动量：惯性和停止

Unfortunately boats don't have brakes so you need to learn to use neutral and to be able to assess how quickly it will stop. Good boat handlers spend a lot of time in neutral just letting the vessel move under its own momentum. All craft when put into neutral will keep moving until the momentum has been lost; this is called 'carrying way'. A large heavy vessel will require more power to make it move in the first place, hence when moving it has greater momentum and will keep moving longer when in neutral.
船都没有刹车，因此要学习如何用空挡位，并能够估计出多久才能把船停住。优秀的操船者大多会利用空挡，让船借助原有动量在惯性下自己移动。所有的船在空挡时都会继续前进直到动量消耗掉而停下来，这就是惯性。大而重的船需要更大的动力来启动，因而其前进的时候也有更大的动量，在空挡的时候也会移动得更远。
Sometimes you may need to use a small amount of engine power to halt the last of this momentum; however it's best to use nature's brakes—the wind and stream.

有时候你可能需要踩倒车油门来耗尽最后的一点动量来停住船；但是最好还是用风和流这些自然力量来刹车。

Because of the combination of wind, stream, and its handling characteristics, a boat is often travelling because of all of these forces. Especially at slow speed it is important to realise that the boat is often not travelling in the direction it is pointing (its heading).

由于风和流的共同作用以及船只的操作特征，船通常是在这些因素的共同作用下前进的。尤其是通常在低速运转时，这些影响更大，一定要认识到低速行进的船因为受到这些因素的影响，航向通常并不是船头所指的方向。

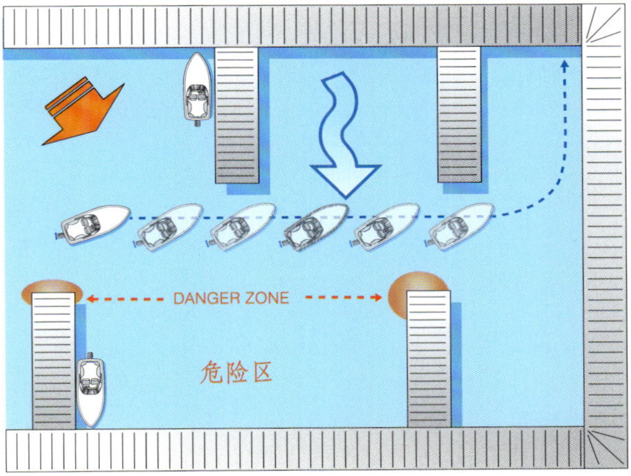

Wind or stream will be trying to move your craft downwind or downstream, therefore it is best to think of all areas downwind or downstream as your ‘Danger Zone’. By knowing which direction stream and wind are trying to take the boat you can use them to your advantage, as nature’s brakes to slow you or to assist you onto a berth. Learning how to read the elements and use them to your advantage is one of the key factors in stress-free boating.

风或流可以把你的船推向下风或下流处，因此应把下风或下流处视作“危险区域”。了解风和流推船的方向，你就可以利用这些影响来发挥你的优势，比如用自然力量刹车来帮助你减速或者靠岸。学习如何了解环境因素以及如何使其为己用非常重要，这是能够轻松驾船的重要因素。

Key to Illustrations: **图例**

Intended route 计划航线

Engine neutral 空挡

Engine ahead 正车

Stream 流

Engine astern 倒车

Wind direction 风的方向

Prop Effect螺旋桨转艏效应

When the engine is put into gear and the propeller turns it provides forward thrust, because of this rotation it also tries to move the stern to one side due to the paddle wheel or 'prop' effect. This affects shaft drive boats more than outboard or sterndrives, in "duoprops" it is almost non-existent. A right handed prop, i.e. one that turns to the right when viewed from behind, in ahead gear tries to walk the stern to the right (starboard). Conversely in astern it tries to walk the stern to the left (port). It is usual for this to be more noticeable in astern gear. If you know what a boat's propeller rotation is you can put this effect to good use when turning and berthing.
把发动机挂上挡位，螺旋桨旋转产生前进推力，由于旋转，桨轮还会产生侧推船尾的力，称之为螺旋桨转艏效应。轴驱动型船比舷外机型船或舷外推动型船的这个效应更明显，但是对于双螺旋桨型船，这个效应几乎没有。右旋螺旋桨，就是那种从后面看往右转的螺旋桨，正车时把船尾往右舷推。对应地倒车时会把船尾往左舷推。往往倒车的时候其效果更为明显。如果你知道螺旋桨旋转的方向，就可以有效地利用这个效应帮助你更好地转向和靠泊。

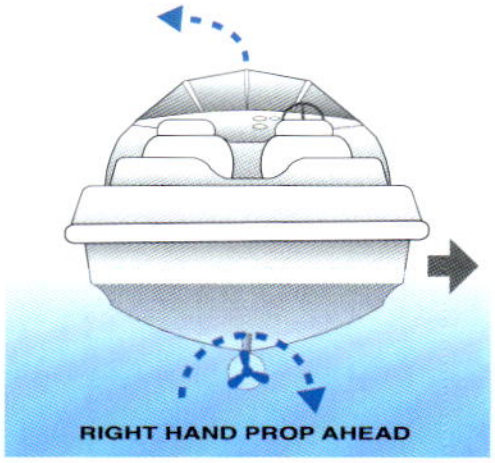

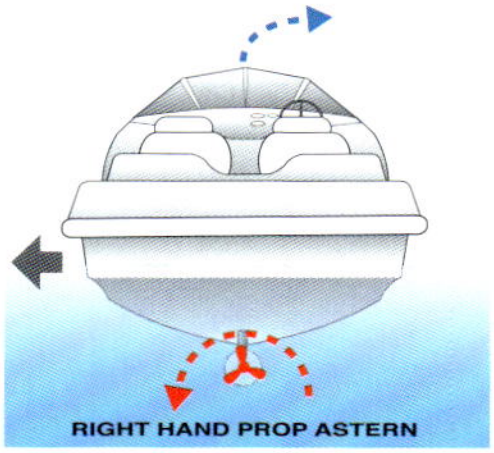

Pivot Points 转向轴心

Boats when going ahead steer from the stern, the pivot point is about one third back from the bow and when you put the wheel hard over to the left (port) and engage ahead gear, roughly one third of the vessel turns to port and the remainder goes to starboard.
船只正车时，转向轴心在距离船头三分之一船长处。如果你正车左满舵，大概三分之一的船身会往左转向，而剩下的部分向右转。
When going astern the pivot point moves aft and when the wheel is hard over to the left (port) with astern gear engaged, one third of the vessel moves to port, the remainder to starboard.
当倒车时，转向轴心向船尾移动。当左满舵倒车时，从船尾到三分之一船长的船身向左转，剩下的部分向右转。
All boats pivot at slightly different points, knowing where the pivot point is on your boat is one of the most important factors in all boat handling exercises.
每艘船的转向轴心都不太一样，了解你的船的转向轴心是所有操船练习中最重要的练习项目。

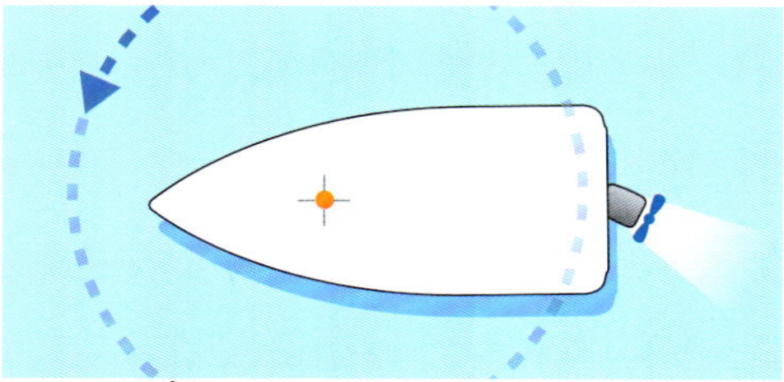
Ahead 正车

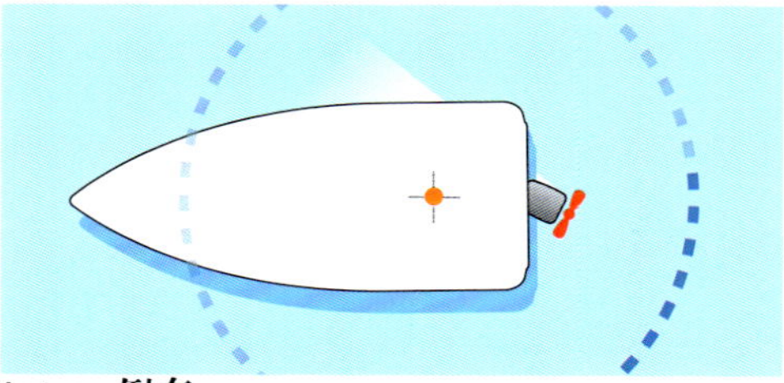
Astern 倒车

Steering 掌舵

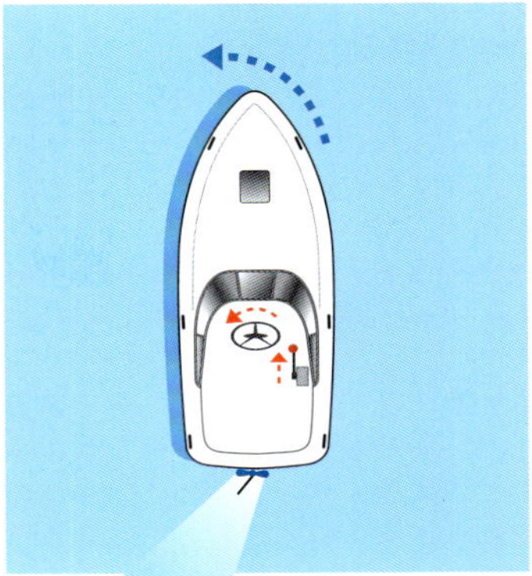

The rudder works by deflecting water passing over it, because it is behind the propeller the effect is much greater when the propeller is turning. At slow speeds a 'burst of power' is very effective as it dramatically increases the water over the rudder without increasing too much speed.
方向舵的作用是使流过舵的水发生偏转，由于它安装在螺旋桨后，因而螺旋桨转动的时候舵效应更大。在低速时，突然加大油门可以显著地提高流过舵的水流而不增加航速，此时舵效应很高。

Outboards and outdrives do not have rudders, they steer by squirting the water in the direction that the drive is turned, as this only happens when it is in gear you need to think 'no gear – no steer'. Because you want the drive in the correct direction before power is applied remember 'wheel before gear'.
舷外机和舷外推动器没有方向舵，它们是通过往驱动器转向的方向喷射水流而转向的。因为只有在挂挡时才会产生舵效，所以你需要记住"无动力-无舵效"。因为你希望在加油之前往正确的方向行驶，所以记住加油前先转舵。

Turning 转向掉头

Steering on boats is not the same as on cars so when turning in a small space you need to take into account all the points above.
操船转向掉头和开车掉头不同，因此在狭小空间转向时，你需要注意以上所有的要点。

Shaft Drive 轴驱动型船

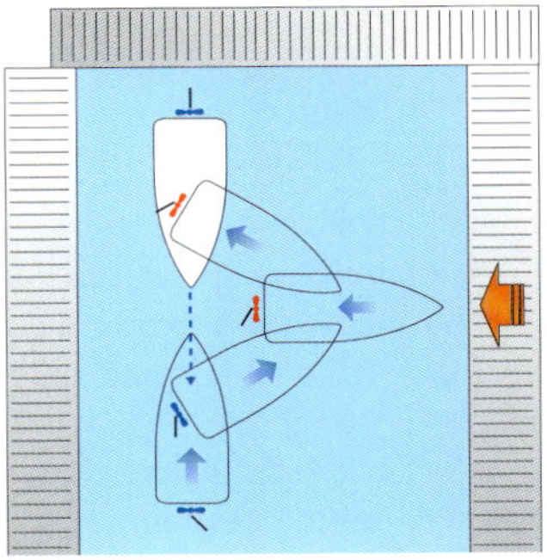

Position the boat roughly in the centre of the space taking into account wind and stream. Approach as slowly as possible, speed carried into the turn will make the turn larger. Turn in the direction that the astern prop effect will assist. Wheel hard over and give a burst ahead, engage neutral. As the rate of turn slows or if space is short give a burst astern; changes in rudder position will have no effect because there is not enough room to gain steerageway. Momentum and prop walk are now turning the boat. Keep this process going until the correct direction is achieved, then select ahead and drive away.
考虑到流和风的影响，把船开到狭小空间的中间位置。在尽可能低速下行驶，因为在高速下转向会导致转弯半径太大。往螺旋桨转艏效应的方向转向。打满舵并突然正车加油，回到空挡。回转速率下降或者空间不够时，突然倒车加一下油门；由于没有足够的空间，打舵无济于事。依靠惯性和螺旋桨侧推效应转动船只。保持这个动作直到得到你需要的掉头方向，正车驶离。

Turning an Outdrive or Outboard
舷外机船或舷外驱动船掉头

Position yourself as for the previous manoeuvre then to turn - wheel hard over to starboard. Engage ahead. Monitor the turn. Neutral when space is short. Wheel hard over to port. Engage astern. Monitor the turn. Neutral when space is short. Straighten wheel, engage ahead and drive out.

和前面一样，第一步是驶到位置，开始转向右满舵，正车，观察转向进度。空间不够时回空挡，左满舵，倒车，观察转向进度。空间不足时回空挡。回正舵，正车驶离。

It is usual to turn into whichever element is strongest, either wind or stream.

通常选择有更强影响的天气条件协助转向，选择顶风或者顶流。

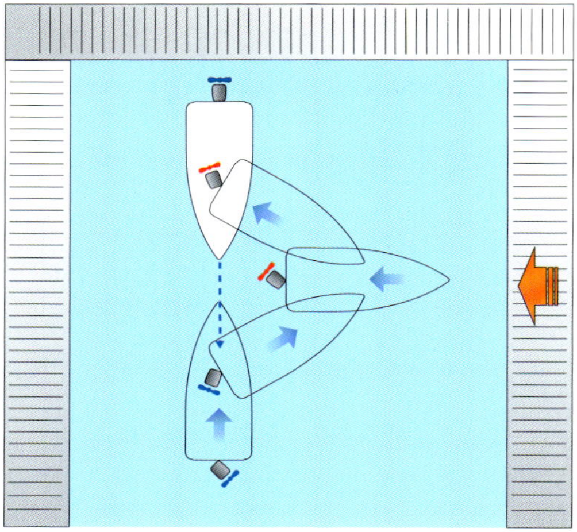

Coming Alongside 靠泊

Outboards and Outdrives 舷外机和舷外驱动型船

Successful manoeuvring between pontoons and other boats is easier if you take account of how your craft reacts. Check what the wind and stream are doing and what effect it will have on your boat and manoeuvre. Approaching into the wind or stream means they can act as a brake. Ideally try to approach using whichever will have the greatest effect. Brief your crew so they know exactly what is expected of them. Prepare fenders and lines. Plan your 'escape' route, just in case the manoeuvre goes wrong.

如果你了解你的船对你的操控会如何反应，在码头和其他船只之间靠泊操作就会很容易。判断风和流的情况以及它们对你的船和操作的影响。顶风顶流行进意味着它们能帮助刹车。理想的情况是利用（风或流）影响最大的因素进行操作。事先通告船员，让他们知晓并理解接下来将要发生什么。准备缆绳和防碰球。计划好放弃靠泊时的驶离路线，以防万一操作失误。

Start your approach as far off the pontoon as is practical. Your angle of approach should be about 30°–40°. Use neutral to keep speed and momentum low. When you are about a boat's length away, steer away from the pontoon and give a touch ahead. This will straighten the boat, try to let the boat stop without using astern. If you are too fast or too steep to the pontoon, steer towards the pontoon and engage astern gear momentarily to bring the boat alongside. This has the effect of slowing you and bringing the stern in. Look sideways to be sure that the boat is stationary.

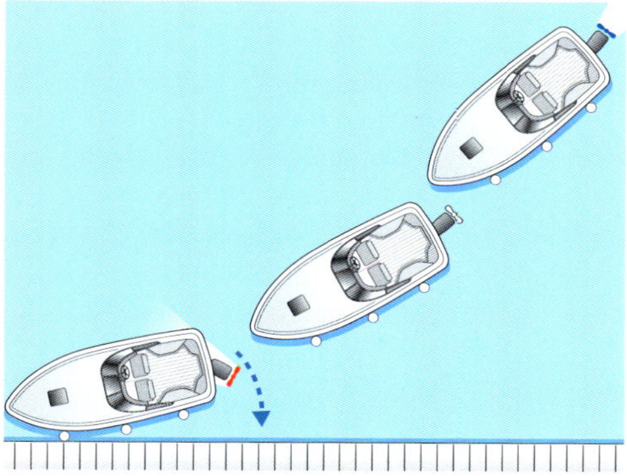

在距离码头尽量远的地方就开始操作。你的靠泊角度应该是与码头成30°～40°。利用空挡保持低速和低动量。到达距离一倍船长处，向驶离码头的方向转舵并正车点一下油门。这样操作将会摆正船身，避免使用倒车停船。如果你的船速太快或者角度太大，向码头方向转舵并用倒挡点油门，这样操作可以把船尾拉向码头，而且能帮助减速。侧向观察确保船停稳。

Shaft Drive **轴驱动型船**

Plan so that you use prop effect to aid berthing. Approach slowly at about 30°. Control speed with neutral and use the rudder to continue steering. As the boat glides alongside engage astern, this will slow the boat and prop effect will pull the stern in.

盘算好，借助螺旋桨侧推效应帮助靠泊的步骤。以30°夹角慢慢前进。用空挡控制好速度，用舵持续控制好方向。当船滑向码头时，换倒挡，这将有助于减速并利用螺旋桨侧推效应把船尾拉靠岸边。

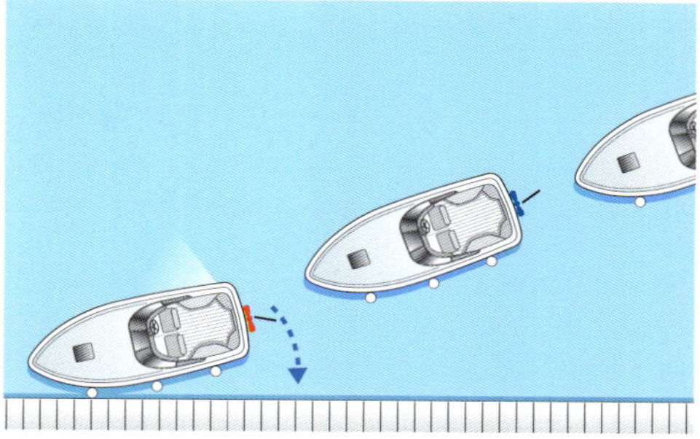

Look sideways to ensure that the boat is stationary. A centre line is very useful to hold a boat on a mooring whilst you sort out the correct mooring lines.

侧向观察确认船只停稳。首先用一根在船中位置的缆绳可以非常有效地把船系在泊位上，接着系其他缆绳。

When wind or stream are making the manoeuvre difficult you will need to be more positive and can also use lines to assist especially on an outboard or outdrive. Motor up to the berth and attach a bow line.Turn the wheel towards the pontoon, engage astern at tick over. The craft will be pulled alongside.

当风或流令操作困难时，你需要保持自信，用缆绳辅助，尤其是对于舷外机或舷外驱动船。开机靠岸系上艏缆。转舵朝向码头方向，以最慢速度倒挡使船尾靠岸。船会靠上码头。

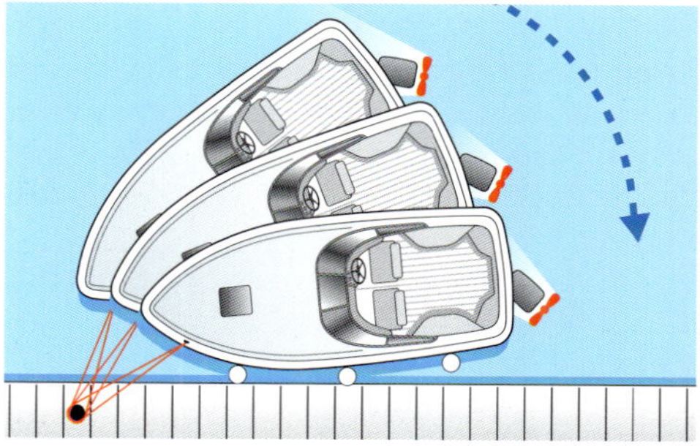

Leaving 驶离

Leaving a pontoon can be a very simple manoeuvre. If the route ahead is clear and there is no wind or stream a good push off the pontoon and driving away in ahead could suffice. However it is usually better to come away in reverse utilising the shape of the boat to roll the bow in first.
驶离泊位是很简单的操作。如果前方路线无障碍，也没有风流的影响，用力推一下然后直接向前驾驶离开码头就可以了。利用船的形状倒船离开通常是更好的选择。

Outboard or Outdrive **舷外机或舷外驱动型船**
Fender the bow, steer towards the pontoon, engage ahead briefly, into neutral, then steer away from the pontoon. Engage reverse and as the stern comes away, straighten up the wheel. Once well clear move off ahead.
用防碰球保护船首，转舵驶向码头方向，前进挡用一点点油门，转回空挡，然后转舵驶向离开码头方向。倒船直到船尾离开，回正舵盘。完全脱离无障碍后驶离码头。

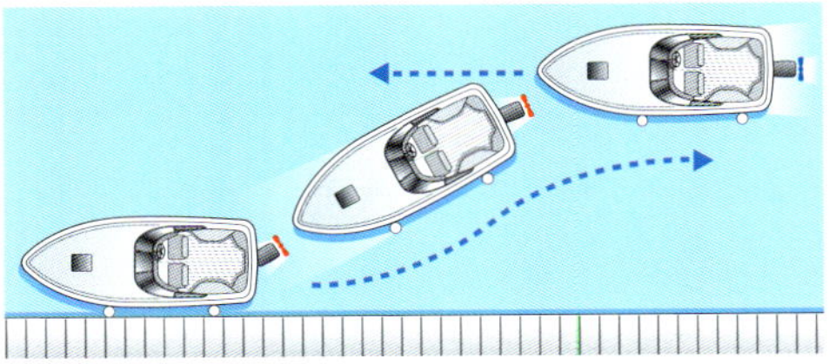

To leave with any wind or stream element holding you on, you may need lines. Decide if you want to leave ahead or astern.
在风或流影响的情况下驶离码头，你需要缆绳辅助。首先需要决定的是先离开船首还是船尾。

Outboard or Outdrives **舷外机或舷外驱动型**

To leave astern—rig a bow line as a slip line and fender the bow area.Turn the wheel away from the dock and engage astern, as the stern comes clear, engage neutral, slip the line and reverse away.
倒车离开：保持系艏缆但可随时滑出松开状态，船首用防碰球保护。向外打舵倒车，当艉离开，回空挡，松艏缆倒车离开。

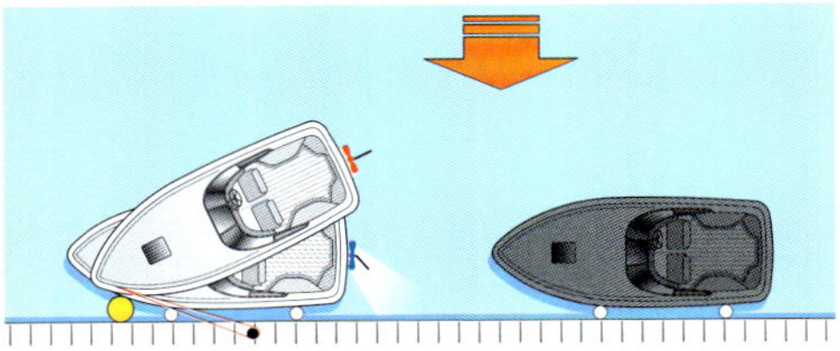

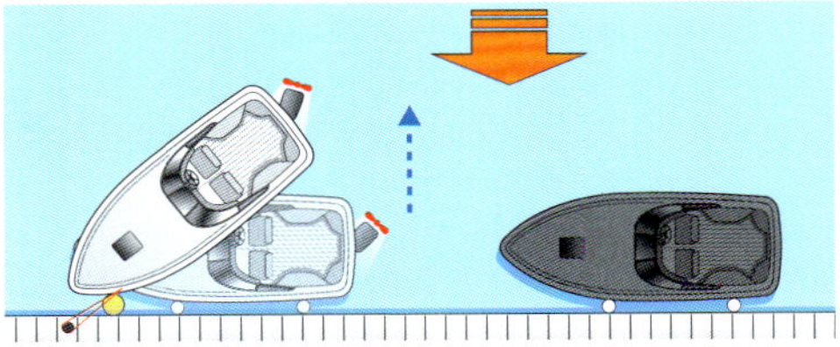

Shaft drive **轴驱动型船**

To leave stern—rig a bow spring as a slip line and fender the bow area.Turn the wheel towards the dock and engage ahead, as the spring tightens this will force the stern out. Engage neutral, slip the line and reverse away.
船尾离开：保持系艏缆并可随时滑出松开状态，船首用防碰球保护，向码头打舵加正车，随着艏缆的拉近，船尾会被推离。回空挡，松艏缆倒车离开。

To leave ahead-all types, rig a stern spring as a slip line. Fender the stern well and engage astern.
船首离开：所有类型的船舶，必须系艉缆并保持随时可松开状态，用防碰球保护船尾倒车。

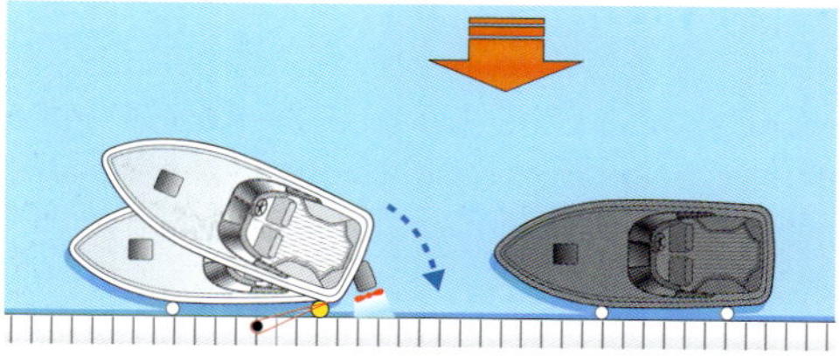

As the spring tightens it forces the bow out. Engage neutral, slip the spring and motor away.
随着艉缆拉紧，船首离开码头，回空挡，松缆绳，开船离开。

Securing the boat **系缆固定船只**

Some small boats are secured with just a single line called the painter (bow line); larger craft may use up to four lines. The bow line (painter) holds the bow to the pontoon and should go forward of the boat. The stern line holds the stern to the pontoon, it should go aft of the boat. The fore (bow) spring stops the boat moving forwards. The aft (stern) spring stops the boat moving backwards.
有些小船只用一根缆绳（通常叫作艏缆）固定，大一些的船最多使用四根缆绳。艏缆固定船首，并向前系在码头上，艉缆固定船尾向后系在码头上，艏倒缆（在船首）防止船往前移动，艉倒缆（在船尾）防止船后移。

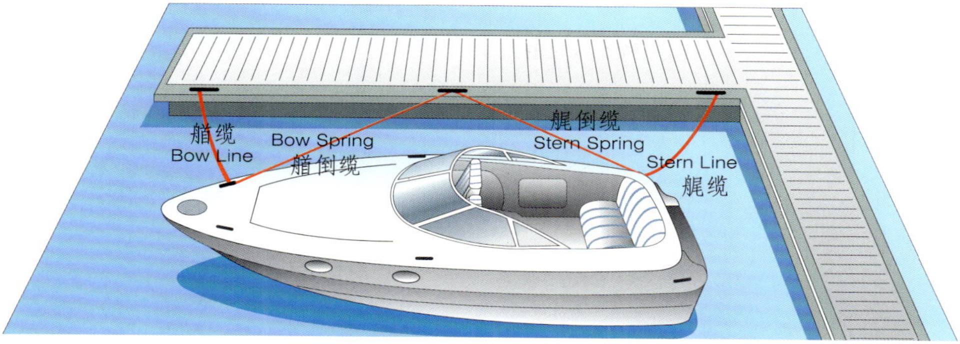

Mooring Buoys 系泊到下锚浮球

Mooring buoys are provided by harbour authorities and clubs, some for short stay (temporary) mooring, others are for longer periods and usually cost less than a pontoon mooring.
码头或俱乐部常提供系泊浮球，有些用于短暂停泊，也有的是为了长期停船，通常其比泊位便宜。

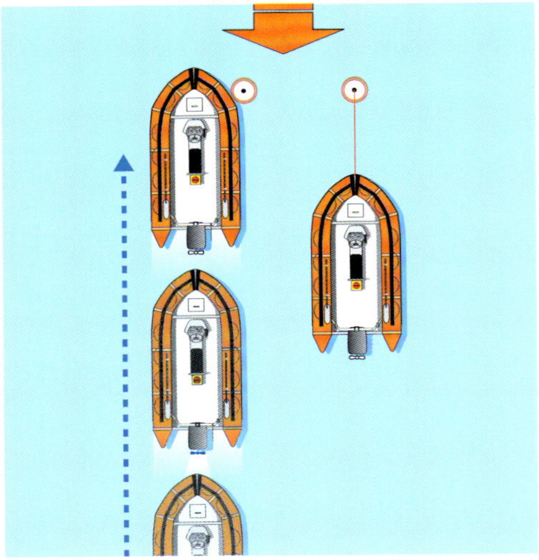

To pick up a mooring buoy: Make sure you know which part of the buoy to make fast to. Watch out for trailing lines on the down-stream side. Tell your crew your intentions, prepare a line early, you may need to use a boat hook. Before you start, plan your escape route. If wind and stream are together approach into them, they will help slow you down. Keep your speed slow, using neutral to control it. Remember to look sideways to help judge your speed. Turn the boat slightly at the last moment to bring the buoy in on the bow area. If wind is against the stream, judge which is the stronger, approach into it, remember you may need to use astern to stop. If using your line to tie off, put at least two turns around the ring to reduce chafe. When using the pick up buoy ensure that you also attach a secure line to the ring.
捡起系泊浮球，确认浮球哪个位置可以挂固定。注意下流方向的尾迹绳。把你的意图告知船员，提前准备好缆绳，你可能需要船钩。开始系泊之前盘算好逃离路线。如果风和流同向，顶风顶流前进，风和流可以帮助减速。保持低速，使用空挡控制。注意侧向观察判断速度。最后一刻轻轻转向，使浮球靠上船首一侧。如果风流不同向，判断哪个影响更强，顶着该条件（风或流）前进，注意你可能需要用倒车停船。如果用你的缆绳套住系泊球上的扣环，至少绕两圈以减少摩损。当使用浮球的绳系泊时，再系一条缆绳作为保险绳。

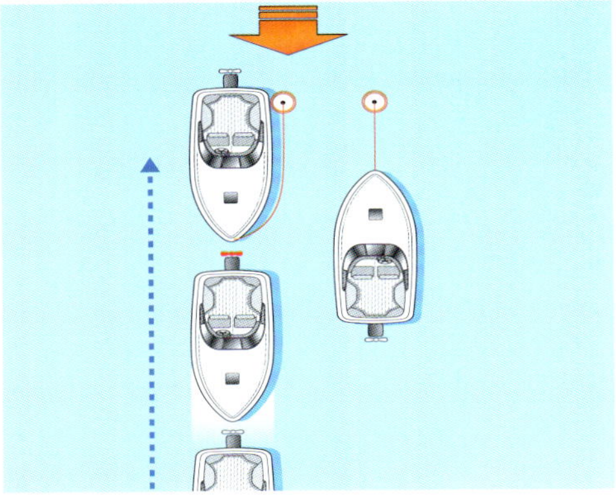

In boats that have high windage or poor bow access, it is often easier to approach stern to the elements. Rig a long line from a bow cleat to the cockpit area. Gently reverse up to the buoy. The long bow line led aft will allow you to tie on as before and the boat will gently swing around, for short stays you can use just a stern line.
如果是风阻很大或者很难在船首工作的船，往往用船尾顶流或风更容易。从艏缆羊角拉长缆绳到驾驶区域，慢慢倒车靠近浮球。利用引到船尾的长艏缆，如同上法系泊，然后让船慢慢掉头。如果只是短暂停留，可以只系艉缆。

Anchoring 锚泊

There are a variety of anchors for small boats, all work well provided that there is enough chain and rope out (scope) for the depth of water. The amount is different when using rope & chain than all chain. An anchor works by having a horizontal pull. On a rope / chain combination the chain acts as a shock absorber, adds weight and reduces chafe.
小型船艇有多种锚，在有足够长锚链或锚绳（锚缆长度与锚的垂直落差比）的情况下都很有效。使用锚绳加锚链组合和只用锚链所需依靠长度不同。锚依靠水平方向的受力来固定船只。在锚绳链组合使用的情况下，锚链部分具有减震的功能，并增加重力和减少摩损。

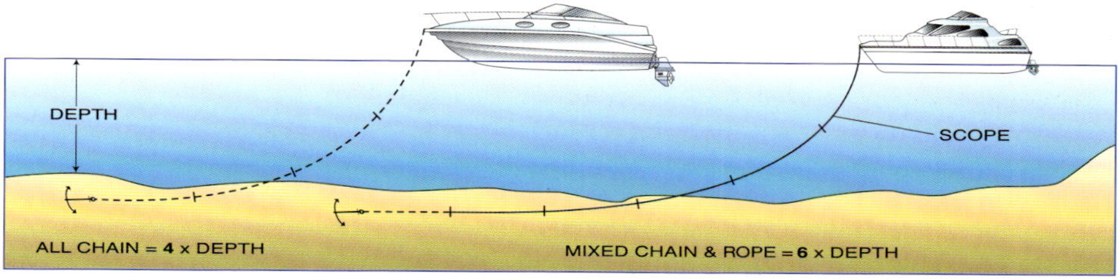

Anchoring is similar to approaching a mooring but without a fixed target. A boat with an open bow area makes it much easier and going forward is simple. On boats with a high foredeck keep one hand holding on at all times.
锚泊和靠浮球系泊类似，但是没有固定的目标位置点。对于艏部开放的船只锚泊很容易，只须前进即可展开工作。在前甲板较高的船上操作时，始终保持一只手抓住护栏以保护个人安全。

Choosing your spot 选择抛锚点

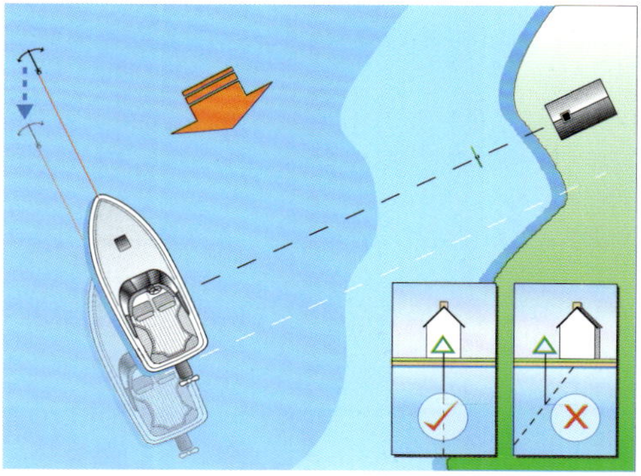

Look for shelter for the duration of your stay. Check the chart for the suitability of the bottom. Consider the rise and fall of the tide, will there be enough water later? How are other craft anchored – will there be enough room to swing? Prepare the anchor and chain / rope for the depth early, secure the end to the boat. Approach as for a mooring, once the boat is stopped lower the anchor to the seabed. Let the wind and stream drift the boat back from the anchor, you may need gentle astern power while your crew feeds out the scope. Check it is holding by engaging astern briefly to dig the anchor in.
Use two objects in line with each other (a transit) ahead and to the side to check you are stationary. If the anchor is dragging raise it and start again. When leaving an anchorage, engage ahead briefly to ease the load, haul in the warp, taking care not

to run over your line. Stow the anchor securely.
在你停留的时段内寻找避风（浪）水域。查询海图确认海床是否适宜抛锚。考虑潮汐落差，确认是否有持续足够的水深，其他抛锚船只的影响——在流向改变后导致船只转动是否还会有足够的安全空间，提前准备好锚和适应水深的锚链、绳，把其一端系在船上。类似系泊法靠近抛锚点，一旦船停下后就可以下锚到海床。让风或流把船往后推漂，水手逐渐放锚缆时，可能还要轻轻地加一点倒车油门。倒车时轻轻加油门可以帮助把锚埋入海床并且确认锚是否锁在海床上了。利用某条连线上的两个固定参考物（叠标法）确认船是否静止，分别检查前面和侧面的叠标。如果走锚了，起锚重新抛锚。离开锚地的时候，轻轻正车卸掉锚链拉力，逐渐把锚链收进绞盘，注意不要拉过了。妥善存储并固定锚。

Collision Regulations 避碰规则

A skipper's decisions as to what action to take at sea are governed by the International Rules for the Prevention of Collisions at Sea (IRPCS). A great deal of the Rules are common sense; for example, you have a responsibility to obey the Rules, keep a good look out, use a safe speed, assess if there is a risk of collision and if so know what to do.
在《国际海上避碰规则》（IRPCS）的约束下，船长决定如何操作。该规则绝大部分的内容都是常识，例如，你有责任遵守该规则，保持瞭望，保持安全速度，判断是否有碰撞风险以及知晓该如何应对。

As a small power boat skipper you give way to all other craft. Other Rules to be aware of are:
作为小型机动艇船长，你需要给其他所有船只避让。
其他需要注意的规则包括：

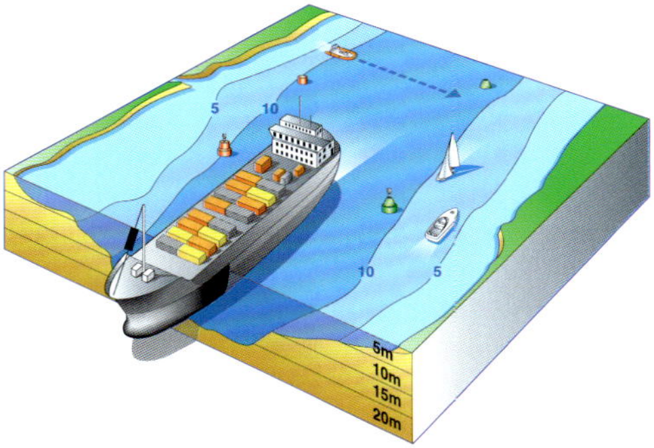

Narrow channels: Do not impede any vessel which requires the depth of water available in the narrow channel.
狭窄水道：不能妨碍任何在狭长水道受水深限制的船只。

Sailing Vessels: Be aware of the Rules for sailing vessels.
帆船：了解帆船规则。

When overtaking: Do not impede any vessel that you are overtaking.
超船：不能妨碍任何你正在超越的船只。

In a head on situation: Both vessels shall alter course and turn to starboard.
正面会船：两条船都要改变航向，向右舷转向。

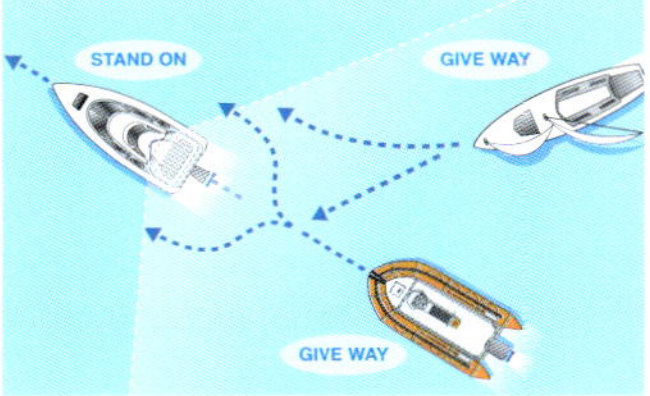

Crossing situations: Give way to traffic coming from the right.
交叉穿越：给右侧的船只让行。

Give way vessel: Take early substantial action.
让路船：尽快采取实质性行动。

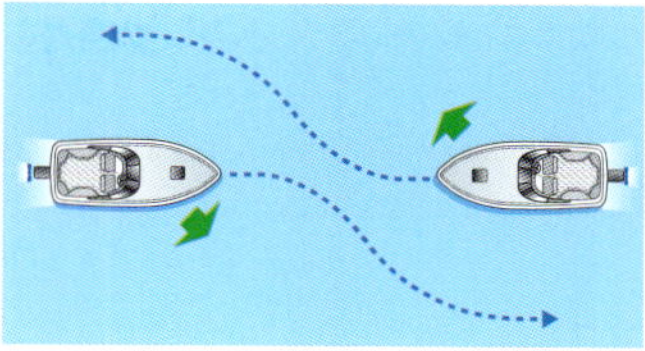

Stand on vessel: Keep your course and speed BUT watch the other vessel; be prepared to take avoiding action.
保持航线船只：保持航向和速度，但要注意瞭望其他船只，随时准备采取避让行动。

Remember at sea no vessel has automatic right of way.
请记住，在海上没有船是必然拥有优先权的。

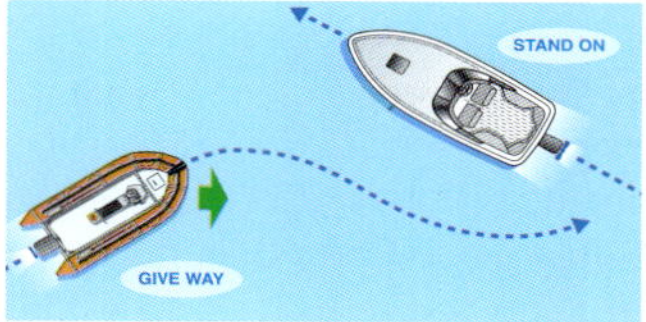

The above Rules only apply to vessels in sight of one another. In poor visibility we are all give way vessels.
以上规则只适用于互相能见的情况下，在能见度不良的情况下我们都是让行船。

Day Shapes and Lights 白天号型和信号灯

By day displaying black shapes identifies a vessel's 'special conditions'. In poor visibility and at night vessels show lights to identify what they are, which direction they are travelling and if they have any special situations.

Fog signals

—— One long blast (4-6 seconds)   ○ One short blast (2 seconds)

	At night	By day
A vessel under 7m and 7 knots. A single white light could also be a vessel at anchor or a vessel seen from astern.		
A powered vessel under 50m shows a white masthead light, a white sternlight and port and starboard lights. Fog —— every two minutes.	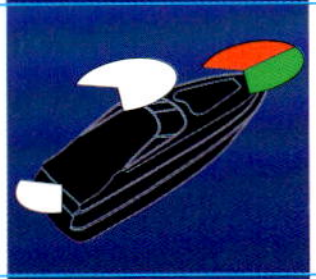	
A powered craft over 50m displays two masthead white lights – the forward one lower than the one at the stern – a white sternlight and its port and starboard lights. Fog —— every two minutes.	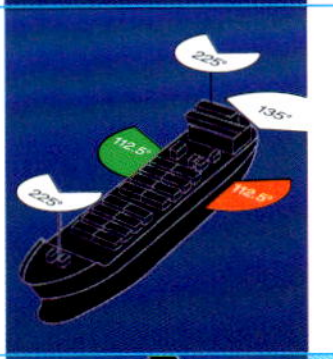	
A yacht under sail either shows a tricolour; or port and starboard lights plus a white sternlight. If the engine is used, it becomes a powered vessel and must display the appropriate lights. Its day shape when motor sailing is a cone pointing downward. Fog —— ○ ○ every two minutes.	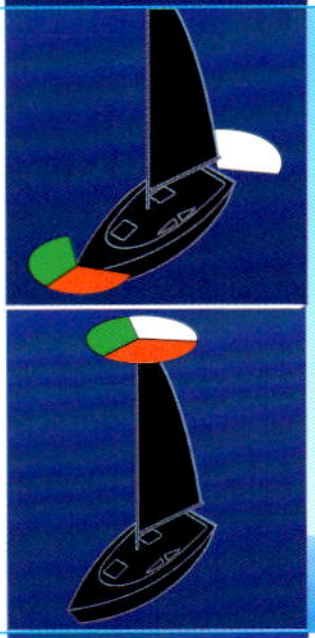	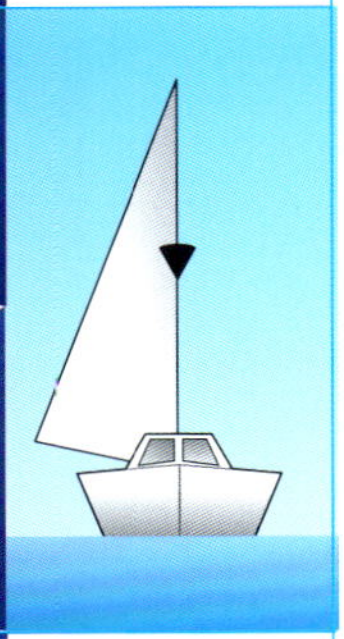
At anchor under 50m only one white light is required. The day shape is a black ball.		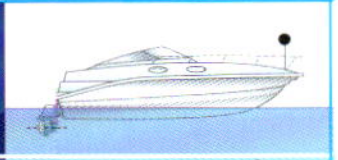
A vessel over 50m at anchor displays two white lights, with the one at the stern lower than the one at the bow. <100m Fog rapid ringing of bell for 5 seconds every minute. >100m Bell rung forward, gong aft for 5 seconds every minute.		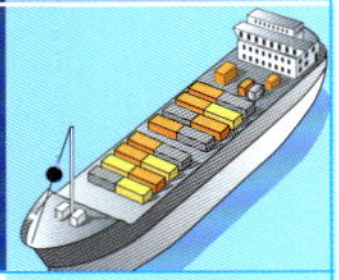
Code flag A indicates a vessel engaged in diving operations – keep well clear at slow speed.		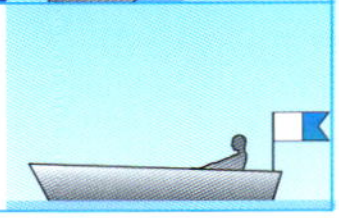

Day Shapes and Lights 白天号型和信号灯

日间航行时使用黑色号型来表示船只的“特殊情况”。在低能见度或者夜晚时，通过信号灯确认船只身份，表示航行的方向和任何其他特殊情况。

雾天信号

—— 一声长鸣（4～6秒） o 一声短鸣（2秒）

	夜晚	白天
船长低于7米且速度低于7节的船舶。一盏白色的信号灯，既能表示锚泊中的船舶，也可能是从船尾看到的船只。		
船长低于50米的动力船应展示一盏白色的桅灯，一盏白色的艉灯和左右舷灯。 雾天：—— 每隔两分钟一声长鸣。	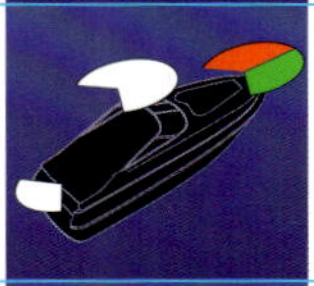	
船长超过50米的动力船舶应展示两盏白色的桅灯，靠近船首的桅灯应稍低于船尾的桅灯——一盏白色的船尾灯和左右舷灯。 雾天：—— 每隔两分钟一声长鸣。	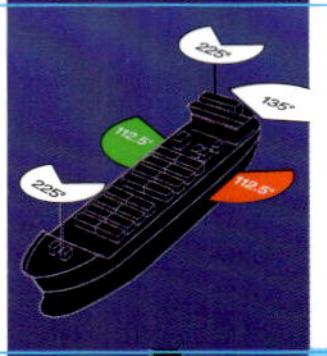	
靠帆行驶的帆船要么展示主桅三色灯，或者左右舷灯加白色的艉灯。当帆船使用发动机航行时，它应该被视为机动艇并适用于该类船舶的信号灯要求。帆机并用航行的帆船的白昼号型是一个倒锥形。 雾天：—— o o 每隔两分钟一声长鸣、两声短鸣。	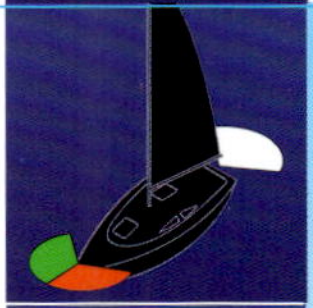 	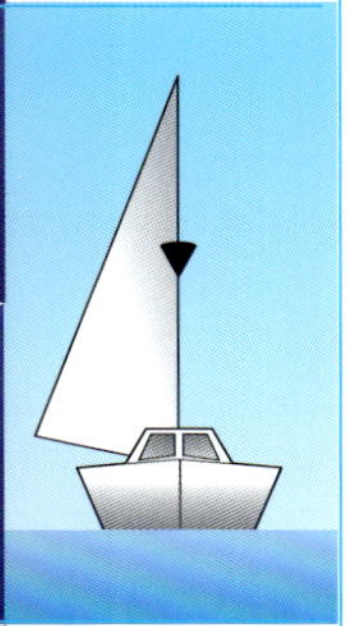
低于50米的船舶，锚泊中的船舶应点亮一盏白灯。白昼号型是一个黑球。 高于50米的船舶，锚泊中的船舶应点亮两盏白灯，靠近船尾的信号灯应稍低于艏信号灯。 低于100米的船舶，雾天应每分钟急敲号钟持续约5秒。 高于100米的船舶，应在船的前部摇铃并紧接着在船尾鸣号锣约5秒，间隔一分钟。	 	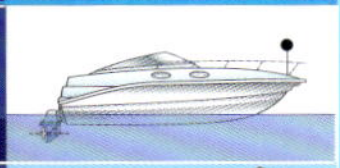 
国际海事信号旗A表示正从事潜水作业的船舶，周围船舶应慢速行驶并注意避让出安全距离。		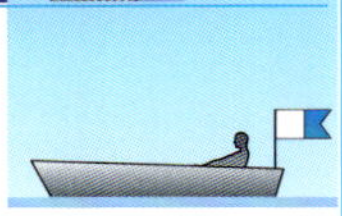

	At night	By day
Vessel engaged in fishing (but not trawling), displays an additional all-round red light above its white light. Two cones apex together by day. Fog —— ○ ○ every two minutes.		
A vessel trawling displays an additional all-round green light above its white light. Two cones apex together by day. Fog —— ○ ○ every two minutes.		
A vessel involved in dredging shows restricted in its ability to manoeuvre, plus two all-round vertical reds to show which side its gear is out and two all-round vertical greens showing the side that is safe to pass. In daylight, diamonds indicate the safe side and balls indicate the side not to pass.	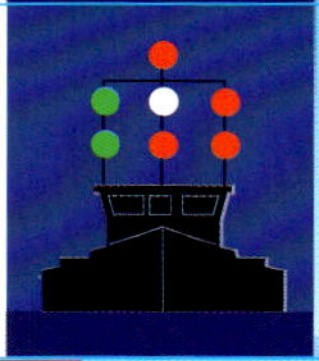	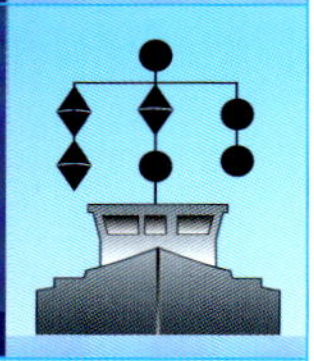
A vessel towing displays an additional white masthead light if the tow is less than 200m, or two additional white masthead lights, if it is greater than 200m. By day diamonds are shown. Fog —— ○ ○ every two minutes. For both types.	 	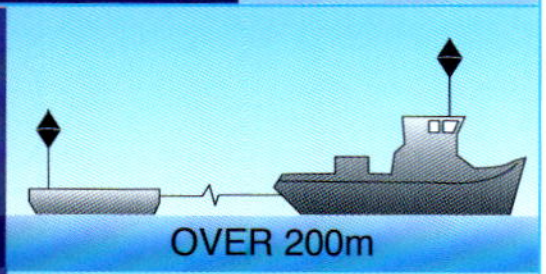 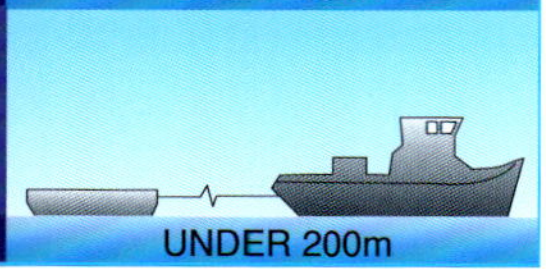

Sounds can be used to indicate what a vessel is about to do. You should have the equipment to make them on board.

One short blast	○	"I am turning to starboard".
Two short blasts	○○	"I am turning to port".
Three short blasts	○○○	"My engines are going astern" – this does not necessarily mean the craft is going backwards.
Five or more short blasts	○○○○○	"I don't understand your intentions" – perhaps better known as "What on earth are you doing?"

	夜晚	白天
正在捕鱼作业（非拖网渔船）的船只，应在白色桅灯之上额外点亮一盏四面可见的红色信号灯。 白昼号型为两个顶端相接的锥体。 雾天：—— ○ ○ 每两分钟一声长鸣两声短鸣。		
拖网渔船应在白色桅灯之上额外点亮一盏四面可见的绿色信号灯。 白昼号型为两个顶端相接的锥体。 雾天：—— ○ ○ 每两分钟一声长鸣、两声短鸣。		
从事挖泥作业的船舶应显示“操作能力受限制”的信号灯，并且应在作业侧的船舷设置两盏四面可见的竖直排列的红色信号灯，在非作业侧的船舷（可安全通过船舷）设置两盏四面可见的竖直排列的绿色信号灯。白天时，菱形号型指示可通过一侧的船舷，球形号型指示不可通过那侧的船舷。		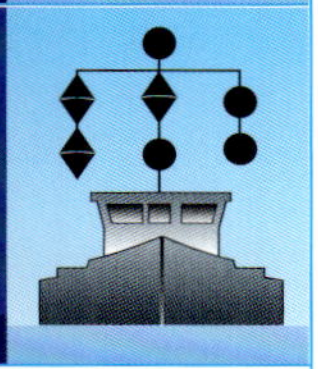
如果整个拖带短于200米，拖引船应点亮额外的一盏白色桅灯。如果拖网长于200米，应展示额外的两盏白色桅灯。白天时展示菱形号型。 雾天：—— ○ ○ 每两分钟一声长鸣两声短鸣。	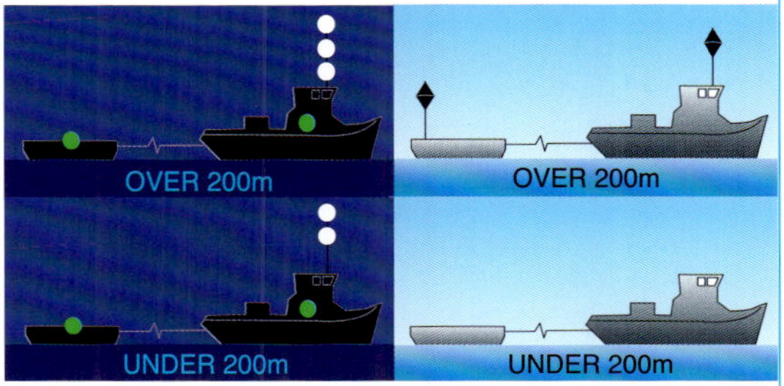	

鸣笛也可用于沟通船舶的下一步动作。你应该在船上安装相关的设备。

一声短鸣 ○	“我要向右舷转向。”
二声短鸣 ○○	“我要向左舷转向。”
三声短鸣 ○○○	“我的发动机倒车”——这并不一定代表船在后退。
四声或更多短鸣 ○○○○○	“我不明白你的意图”——“你到底在做什么？”

Man Overboard
人员落水

If Someone Goes Overboard 如果有人落水

- Alert the rest of the crew by shouting ‘Man overboard’.
  应大声地提醒提醒其他船员“有人落水”。
- Instruct one person to point at the MOB at all times.
  指定一位船员在船上用手一直指向落水人员。
- At slow speed, continue straight until well clear of the MOB.
  低速直行，直到完全离开落水人员。
- Make a slow controlled turn towards the MOB ensuring you have enough room so as not to run them over.
  缓慢转向落水人员并留出足够空间避免撞到人。
- If you are in danger of running over the MOB, abandon the manoeuvre and start again.
  如果有撞到落水人员的危险，请放弃本次操纵，重新开始。
- Your approach will be governed by the wind and is similar to that of approaching a mooring buoy (see page 28) without the stream element.
  靠近（落水人员）时会受到风的影响，这与接近没有水流影响的系泊浮球相似（见第28页）。

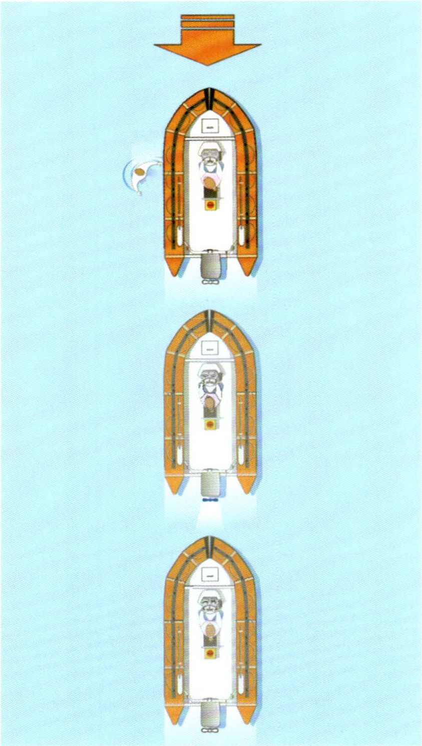

Approaching a MOB 接近落水人员

There are two methods that work in Small Craft to recover a MOB:
对于小型船舶，有两种方法营救落水人员：

Method 1 方法一

Decide which side to pick up the casualty.
On small boats this should be the opposite side to the controls. Start the approach from downwind. Slowly move the boat towards the casualty. Use neutral to manage your speed.
Aim to bring the MOB onto your windward bow. When the MOB is near, remove power and grab hold of the MOB. Switch off the engine*. Manhandle the MOB to an area of the boat where you can recover them.
决定从哪一边来救起落水人员。对于小型船舶来说，应该选择油门挡位操控杆的另一侧。首先，从下风处靠近，慢速把船转向落水人员。使用空挡控船。尽量从迎风的船头位置救起落水人员。当靠近落水人员时，关油门并抓住落水人员。熄灭发动机。把落水人员安置到船上易于实施下一步急救的区域。

Advantages 优点

Good for craft with low freeboards. Allows waves to be taken head-on. Good if rough as MOB is unlikely to go under the boat.
适用于干舷较低的船舶。可以让船头顶浪。风浪较大时，落水人员不易被卷入船底。

Disadvantages 缺点

Can be difficult if you are alone. You can lose sight of the MOB under the bow. You will need to be very quick at collection time.
单人不易操作。可能会被船头遮挡视线而看不到落水人员。需要在适当的时机迅速地从水中捞起落水人员。

Method 2 方法二

This time go upwind of the MOB. Stop and position your boat beam on upwind of the MOB. Keep adjusting your position to drift down onto the MOB. When alongside switch off engine.*
从上风处接近落水人员。调整船舶，尽量使船侧舷保持在落水人员的上风处。持续调整船的位置，横移靠近落水者。当落水人员在船侧时，熄灭发动机。*

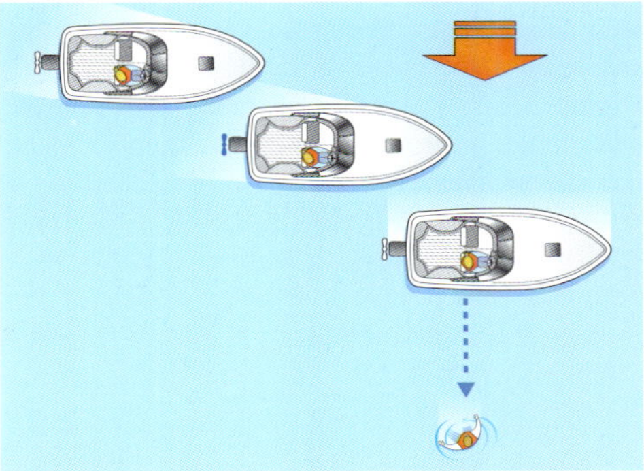

Advantages 优点

Suits high sided vessels where sight of the MOB is easily lost when approaching them into the wind. Provides some shelter to the MOB. Allows the boat to be brought alongside the MOB at the cockpit area where the freeboard is lowest. Bringing a MOB in on the leeward (downwind) side makes the boat lower in the water and so aids recovery.
适用于船舷较高的船舶。对这种船舶来说，当在顶风靠近落水人员时，因为视线被遮挡，极易失去落水人员的定位。船体给落水人员提供的一定的遮挡风浪的作用。可以使驾驶位区域的船舷靠近落水人员，此处的干舷最低。从下风处救起落水人员，这一侧的干舷更低，易于救援。

Disadvantages 缺点

Can be uncomfortable being beam-on to the sea. Craft can be blown over the top of the MOB.
横浪下摇摆严重会令人员不舒适。船舶可能会被风浪横推撞向落水人员。

* As a skipper you need to balance the clear safety benefits of switching off the engine against the sea conditions and the location you are in. However, on RYA courses you will be expected to demonstrate best practice by switching the engine off. A MOB is a very serious situation, you should be prepared to call a MAYDAY if you have any doubt in your ability to recover the casualty.
*作为船长，你需要从安全的角度权衡何时关闭发动机和如何合适地定位船舶。但是，在RYA的课程中会让你演示正确地关闭发动机。人员落水是非常危险的情况，当你不确定能否独自完成救援时，你应准备呼叫“Mayday”。

Summonning Assistance 呼叫救援

There are several ways that you can summon assistance to your boat; however you need first to assess how serious the problem is, and what help you require. If you, your boat or your crew are in immediate danger you must send out a Mayday call. This can be sent by a VHF (DSC) Mayday call, mobile phone, arm signals (if there are vessels close by), sounding your horn etc. or by using flares.
有几种方法可以呼叫救援，当然首先你需要判断问题有多严重，以及你需要什么样的帮助。如果你、你的船或你的船员面临紧急的危险，你必须马上发出求救信号（Mayday）。这可以通过甚高频无线电对讲机（数字选择和呼叫终端信号DSC）的Mayday信号、手机、挥手（如果附近有船只）、吹号或者使用烟雾弹等火焰信号。

Mayday Call 求救呼叫

How this is sent will depend slightly on the equipment, however the basic principles on a DSC radio are: remove the cover to the 'Distress' button, press and hold it for 5 seconds. This will broadcast a Digital Alert to all DSC equipped craft and the local coastguard. If properly programmed the alert will include your MMSI (a unique number identifying your craft) your position, the time and can also include the nature of the distress. You can follow up this DSC alert with a voice Mayday call as shown.
根据设备不同，发信号的方法略有不同，但是DSC广播的基本步骤都是：打开求救（Distress）按钮的盖，按住5秒。这时广播会发布一个数字求救信号给所有装备了DSC设备的船只和附近的海岸警卫队。如果步骤正确，求救信号会包括你的海上移动通信识别码（MMSI，船舶的唯一识别编号）和你的位置、时间以及危险性质。你可以继续用这个DSC信号发布如下语音求救（Mayday）信号。

Mayday, Mayday, Mayday	Mayday, Mayday, Mayday (呼救信号)
This is powerboat	这是机动艇
Beta, Beta, Beta	Beta，Beta，Beta
Callsign MYFT6 MMSI 234001234	呼号MYFT6MMSI 234001234
Mayday Beta	Mayday Beta
My position is 50° 30′.5N, 001° 57′.5W	我的位置是北纬50° 30′.5,西经001° 57′.5
Have hit submerged object and am sinking. We require immediate assistance.Four persons on board	撞到半潜漂浮物，正在下沉。我们需要紧急救助。船上四人正在弃船登救生筏。
Abandoning to the life raft.	
Over.	结束。

Now release the transmit button to receive a reply by voice. If you hear a Mayday do not use your radio unless you can offer assistance as you may mask vital transmissions. If you do not have a DSC radio use the voice procedure given above.
现在需要松开发送按键，才能收到语音回复。如果你听到求救信号（Mayday），除非你能提供援助，否则不要使用收音机，因为你可能会屏蔽重要信号。如果你没有DSC对讲机，使用上图的语音程序。

Mobile phone 手机

Mobiles can be used for requesting help, however they do have drawbacks, such as limited range in many coastal locations and only one person hears your call. Additionally, they cannot be homed in on as easily as a VHF transmission. A text message may stand a better chance of getting through.
可以使用手机求救，但是它有缺点，比如手机覆盖范围有限，而且只有一个人能接听到你的电话。另外，与甚高频无线电传输相比，它的信号没有那么容易收到。短信传输成功的概率会更大。

Flares 信号弹

Flares are an essential part of boating equipment; however there are several different types and you need to ensure you know how to use them before an emergency arises.
信号弹是船上必备的装备，其有很多种，你需要在紧急情况发生前就知晓如何使用它。
All flares are held and fired downwind and don't last forever, so check the expiry dates and dispose of old flares safely (see manufacturer's instructions).For further guidance on distress signals visit the RYA website.
所有信号弹都是手持并向下风射出的，它们都有有效期，因此要检查有效期并安全处理过期信号弹（根据制造商说明书处置）。有关遇险信号的进一步指导，请访问RYA网站。

	Recommended number to carry	建议配备的数量	Inshore 近岸	Sheltered waters 避风浪水域
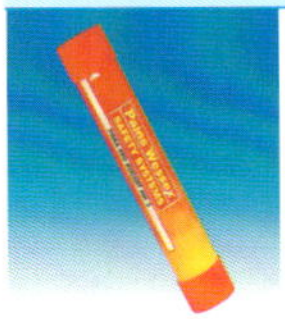	Red parachute flare The most effective long range flare; projects a bright flare to about 300m. Do not use near helicopters!	红色降落伞信号弹 最有效的大范围火焰信号，可以把火焰信号发射到300米高。不要在直升机旁发射！	任意	0
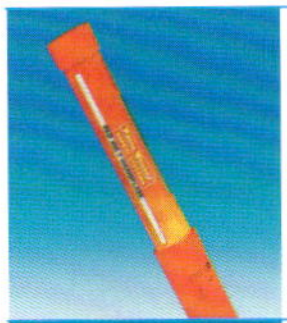	Red hand-held flare Indicates precise position of craft, use when close to other craft or land.	红色手持火焰信号弹 可以指示船只的准确位置，附近有船只或靠近岸边时使用。	3	2
	Orange hand-held smoke Use in daylight, useful for attracting helicopter or lifeboat attention.	橙色手持烟雾弹 日间（能见度良好）使用，有效地获得直升机或者救生艇的注意。	2	2

Fire 防火

Many small boats are petrol powered, therefore it is sensible that you carry a fire extinguisher on board and you and your crew know how to use it. Most marine extinguishers use powder which is good at extinguishing electrical or flammable liquid fires. They work by smothering the fire, and therefore you must aim at the base of the fire. Fire blankets are also very good.
很多小船都是用燃油发动机推进的，因此在船上放一个灭火器，并且保证你和你的船员知道如何使用是非常有用的。大多海事灭火器都可以有效地扑灭电路或可燃液体火灾。其工作原理是阻隔空气灭火，因此你必须对准燃烧火焰的根部。灭火毯也是很好用的。

If you do not need urgent help e.g. you have run out of fuel and are not drifting into immediate danger your call for assistance can be made to another vessel or the coastguard.
如果你不需要紧急帮助，比如你没有燃油了并且没有漂流向危险地带，你可以向其他船只或者海岸警卫队求助。

Navigation 导航

Charts 海图

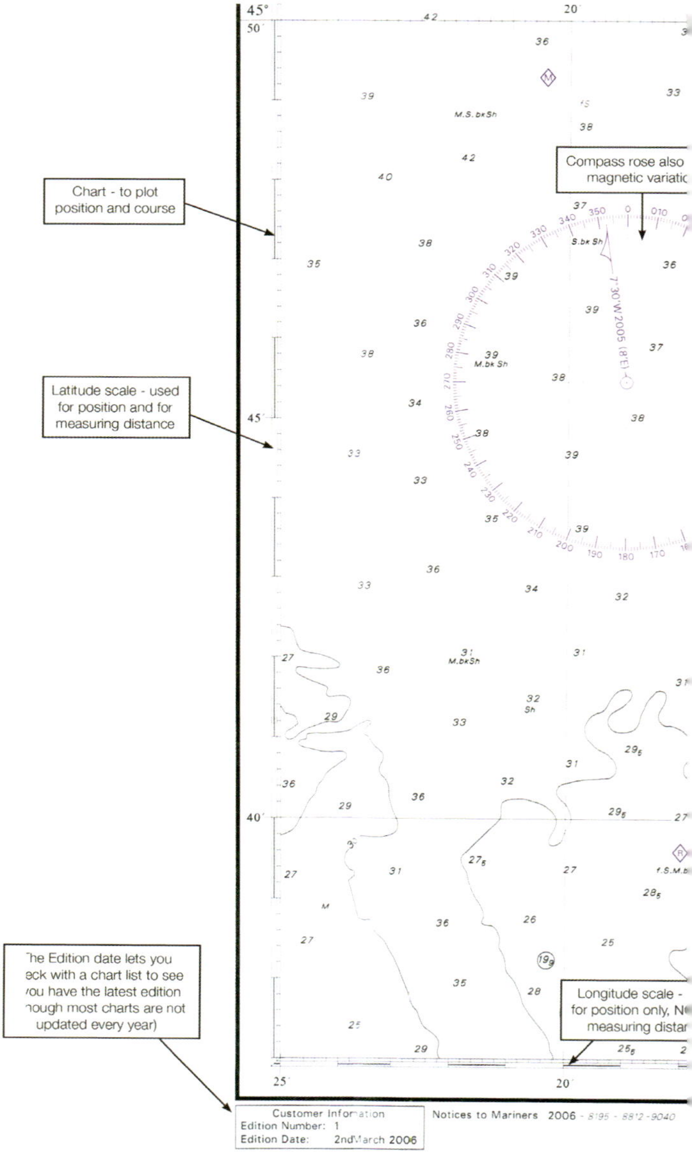

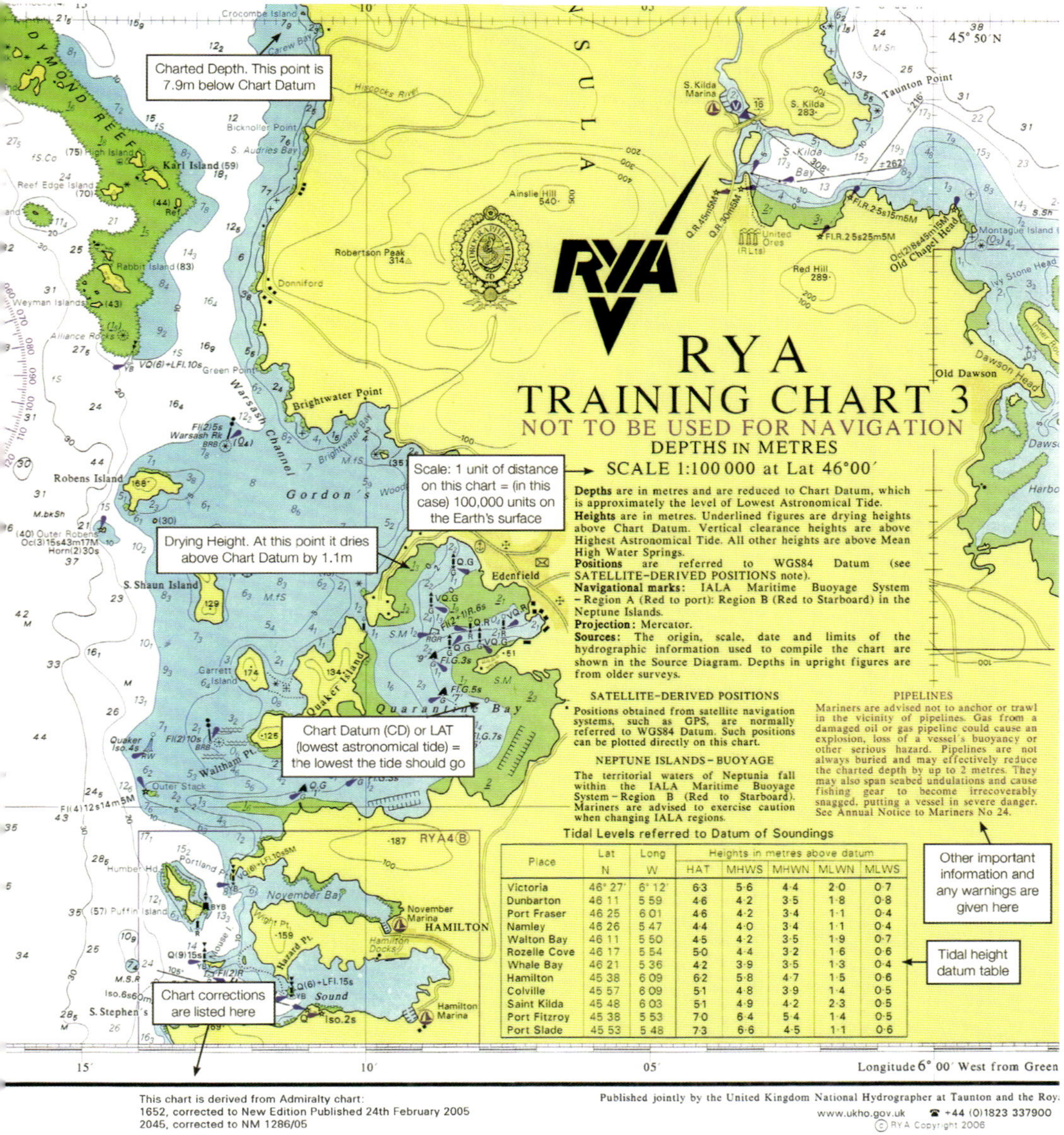
Charted Depth. This point is 7.9m below Chart Datum
Scale: 1 unit of distance on this chart = (in this case) 100,000 units on the Earth's surface
Drying Height. At this point it dries above Chart Datum by 1.1m
Chart Datum (CD) or LAT (lowest astronomical tide) = the lowest the tide should go
Chart corrections are listed here
Other important information and any warnings are given here
Tidal height datum table
RYA
TRAINING CHART 3
NOT TO BE USED FOR NAVIGATION
DEPTHS IN METRES
SCALE 1:100 000 at Lat 46°00′
Depths are in metres and are reduced to Chart Datum, which is approximately the level of Lowest Astronomical Tide.
Heights are in metres. Underlined figures are drying heights above Chart Datum. Vertical clearance heights are above Highest Astronomical Tide. All other heights are above Mean High Water Springs.
Positions are referred to WGS84 Datum (see SATELLITE-DERIVED POSITIONS note).
Navigational marks: IALA Maritime Buoyage System – Region A (Red to port): Region B (Red to Starboard) in the Neptune Islands.
Projection: Mercator.
Sources: The origin, scale, date and limits of the hydrographic information used to compile the chart are shown in the Source Diagram. Depths in upright figures are from older surveys.
SATELLITE-DERIVED POSITIONS
Positions obtained from satellite navigation systems, such as GPS, are normally referred to WGS84 Datum. Such positions can be plotted directly on this chart.
NEPTUNE ISLANDS – BUOYAGE
The territorial waters of Neptunia fall within the IALA Maritime Buoyage System – Region B (Red to Starboard). Mariners are advised to exercise caution when changing IALA regions.
PIPELINES
Mariners are advised not to anchor or trawl in the vicinity of pipelines. Gas from a damaged oil or gas pipeline could cause an explosion, loss of a vessel's buoyancy or other serious hazard. Pipelines are not always buried and may effectively reduce the charted depth by up to 2 metres. They may also span seabed undulations and cause fishing gear to become irrecoverably snagged, putting a vessel in severe danger. See Annual Notice to Mariners No 24.
Tidal Levels referred to Datum of Soundings
Place | Lat N | Long W | Heights in metres above datum: HAT | MHWS | MHWN | MLWN | MLWS
Victoria | 46° 27′ | 6° 12′ | 6·3 | 5·6 | 4·4 | 2·0 | 0·7
Dunbarton | 46 11 | 5 59 | 4·6 | 4·2 | 3·5 | 1·8 | 0·8
Port Fraser | 46 25 | 6 01 | 4·6 | 4·2 | 3·4 | 1·1 | 0·4
Namley | 46 26 | 5 47 | 4·4 | 4·0 | 3·4 | 1·1 | 0·4
Walton Bay | 46 11 | 5 50 | 4·5 | 4·2 | 3·5 | 1·9 | 0·7
Rozelle Cove | 46 17 | 5 54 | 5·0 | 4·4 | 3·2 | 1·6 | 0·6
Whale Bay | 46 21 | 5 36 | 4·2 | 3·9 | 3·5 | 1·3 | 0·4
Hamilton | 45 38 | 6 09 | 6·2 | 5·8 | 4·7 | 1·5 | 0·6
Colville | 45 57 | 6 09 | 5·1 | 4·8 | 3·9 | 1·4 | 0·5
Saint Kilda | 45 48 | 6 03 | 5·1 | 4·9 | 4·2 | 2·3 | 0·5
Port Fitzroy | 45 38 | 5 53 | 7·0 | 6·4 | 5·4 | 1·4 | 0·5
Port Slade | 45 53 | 5 48 | 7·3 | 6·6 | 4·5 | 1·1 | 0·6
Robens Island
S. Shaun Island
Quaker Island
Gordon's Wood
Quarantine Bay
Edenfield
Brightwater Point
Warsash Channel
Karl Island (59)
Rabbit Island (83)
DYMOND REEF
Robertson Peak 314
Ainslie Hill 540
Red Hill 289
S. Kilda Marina
S. Kilda 283
Taunton Point
Old Chapel Head
Montague Island
Old Dawson
Dawson Head
November Bay
November Marina
HAMILTON
Hamilton Marina
Portland Pt
Hazard Pt.
Waltham Pt.
Humber Hd
Outer Stack
S. Stephen's
Sound
RYA4
45° 50′N
Longitude 6° 00′ West from Green
This chart is derived from Admiralty chart:
1652, corrected to New Edition Published 24th February 2005
2045, corrected to NM 1286/05
Published jointly by the United Kingdom National Hydrographer at Taunton and the Roy
www.ukho.gov.uk ☎ +44 (0)1823 337900
© RYA Copyright 2006

Position 定位

Charts are the nautical equivalent of maps. The information they show allows you to navigate safely.
海图就是适用于航海需求的地图。海图的信息能够帮助你安全航行。

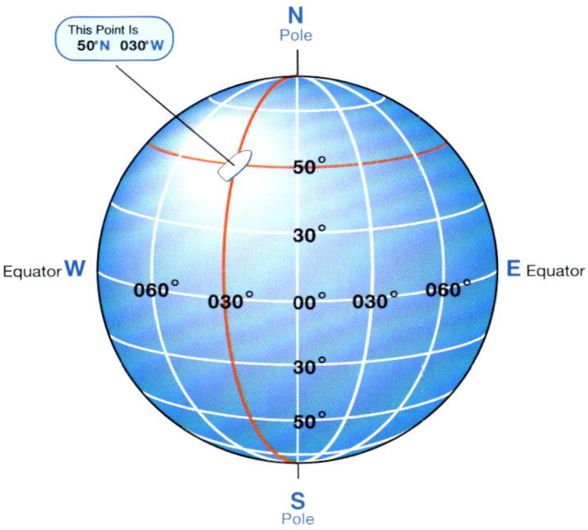

To define precise position on the Earth’s surface two imaginary lines are ‘drawn’ on the Earth. Longitude lines run North-South between the poles. Latitude lines run horizontally around the Earth parallel to the equator.
为了在地球表面精确定位，在地球上“画”了两条假想的线。经线通过两极点贯穿南北，纬线平行于赤道水平环绕地球。

Where these lines intersect gives a position like on the globe shown, this position is expressed in degrees either North or South of the equator and East or West of the Prime Meridian. The position on the globe is thus: 50° 00′.0 N, 030° 00′.0 W
这些线的交叉点给出了位置信息，就好像在上图这个地球上看到的那样，这个位置信息通过在赤道南或北的度数、本初子午线的东或西边的度数表示。这个地球范例上的位置可以表达为北纬 50° 00′.0（北纬50度0分0秒），西经 030° 00′.0（西经30度，0分0秒）。

Each degree can be divided into fractions of a degree. Like hours, a degree consists of 60 minutes, and each minute consists of 60 seconds. Seconds are now usually expressed as decimals, so 42′ 30′′ becomes 42′ 5.
度可以分为度数和分数，就好像一个小时时间，一度包括60分，一分包括60秒。这里秒常通过十进制表示，于是42′ 30′′ 就是42.5′。

On the globe, the craft is 50 degrees north (50°N); one degree of latitude equals 60 nautical miles, therefore since one minute of latitude equals one nautical mile (equals 1852m on land), in this example, 50° × 60 miles = 3000 miles North of the Equator.
在地球上，船在北纬50°；一纬度的距离等于60海里。于是纬度的1分等于1海里（约为1852米），在这个例子中里，50° ×60 海里 = 3000 赤道以北3000海里。

For chartwork we use plotting symbols to make things clear:
对于海图，我们使用标绘符号来表示特定事物：

Fix 地物

Water track 水面航迹

Waypoint (WPT) 航路点

Ground track 地面航迹

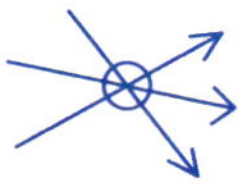
Fix from visual bearings
对地物的目测方位角

Tidal set and drift 潮汐海流

A chart is only accurate on the day it is printed. Harbour authorities may move, add or remove buoys. Always check in the bottom left hand corner of the chart to see when it was last updated. Regular correction notices are published, and from these you should update your charts.
海图只有在打印那天是准确的，因为港口机构可能会移动，航标会增加或移除。建议经常检查海图左下角注释的该图的更新日期。有关机构会定期出版修正，你应当及时更新你的海图。

Measuring distance on a chart
在海图上测量距离

When measuring distance, always take the dividers to the 'latitude' scale on the side of the chart alongside the area that you are measuring.
测量距离的时候，请用圆规对照你要测量海图旁侧的纬度刻度。

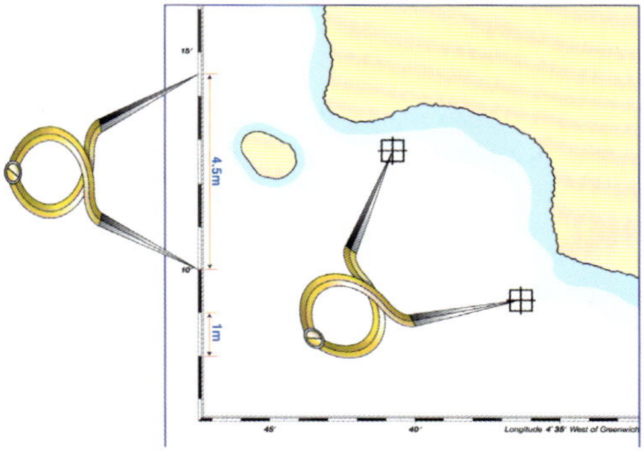

Plotting a Position
绘制位置点

To plot a position on a chart from a latitude and longitude, mark off the latitude by marking a horizontal line in the rough area you expect it to intersect the meridian of longitude.
利用经度和纬度在海图上绘制位置，在期望能与对应经线交叉的大概区域内画一条水平线标出该位置的纬度。

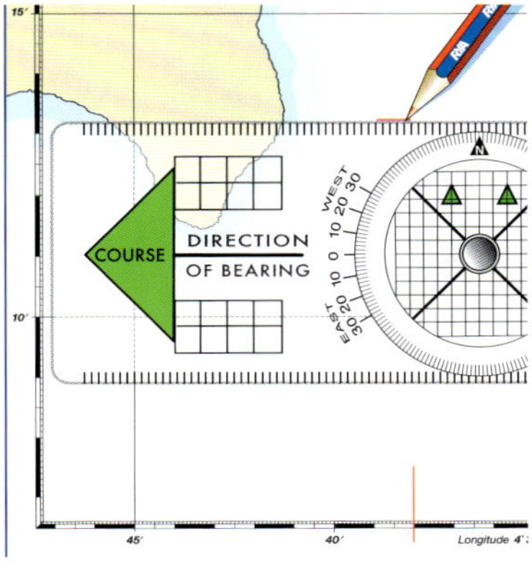

Then mark off the meridian of longitude from the scale at the top or bottom of the chart.
然后根据在图顶或图底的刻度画出垂直的经线。

Where the lines intersect is the position.
交叉点就是所需位置。

When plotting you can either use a plotter or dividers. A plotter is easier on a small powerboat.
绘图时，你可以使用圆规或者绘图尺，绘图尺在小型船只上很方便使用。

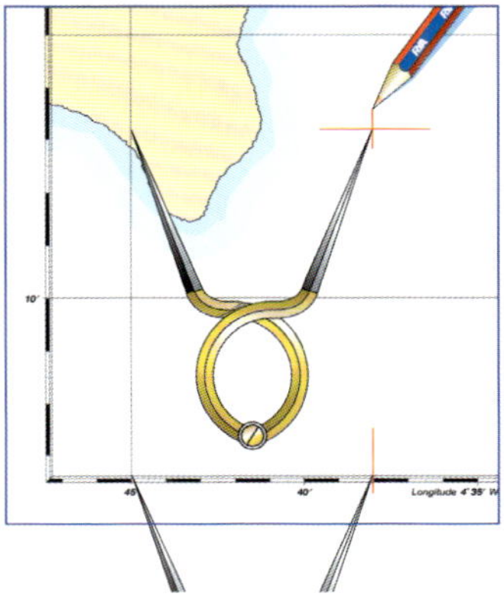

Tides 潮汐

Tides are the changing depth of water above chart datum, more generally referred to as the vertical change in sea level - up and down. They are caused by the gravitational effect of the Moon and the Sun on the Earth and run roughly on a 28 day cycle with two 'Spring' and 'Neap' periods in each cycle.
潮汐是海图基准水平面上水深的变化情况，一般用海平面的垂直高度变化（上和下）标识。潮汐是由于月球和太阳与地球的引力产生的。一般以28天为一个周期，每个周期内有两次大潮、两次小潮。

Spring tides: when the Earth is in line with the Moon and Sun and the gravitational effect is at its greatest, this gives high tides at their highest, and low tides at their lowest.
大潮：当地球、太阳、月球近乎在同一条线上时，引力叠加，影响最大，因而海面升降幅度最大，这个时候的高潮位更高，低潮位更低。

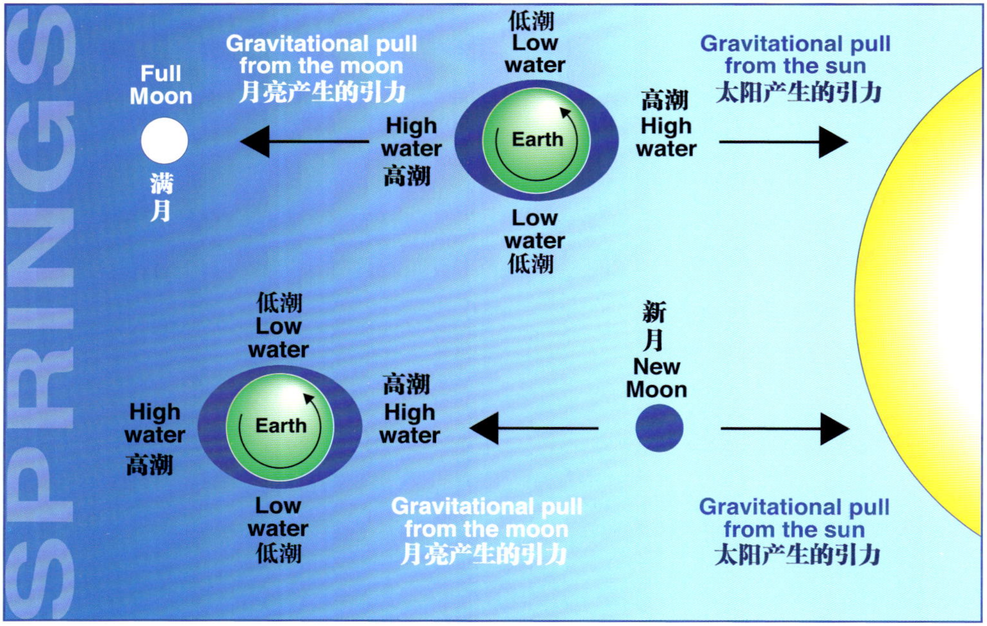

Neap tides: when the gravitational pull of the moon and the sun are split roughly at right angles the result is, the highs are less high and the lows are less low than at spring tides.
小潮：当月球和太阳相对地球的引力方向近似成直角的时候，引力叠加作用使海面升降幅度较小，高潮位比大潮时低，低潮位比大潮时高。

In between these extremes we have constantly changing value depending where we are in the cycle.
在这两个极限位置之间，潮汐高度周期性地随时间变化。

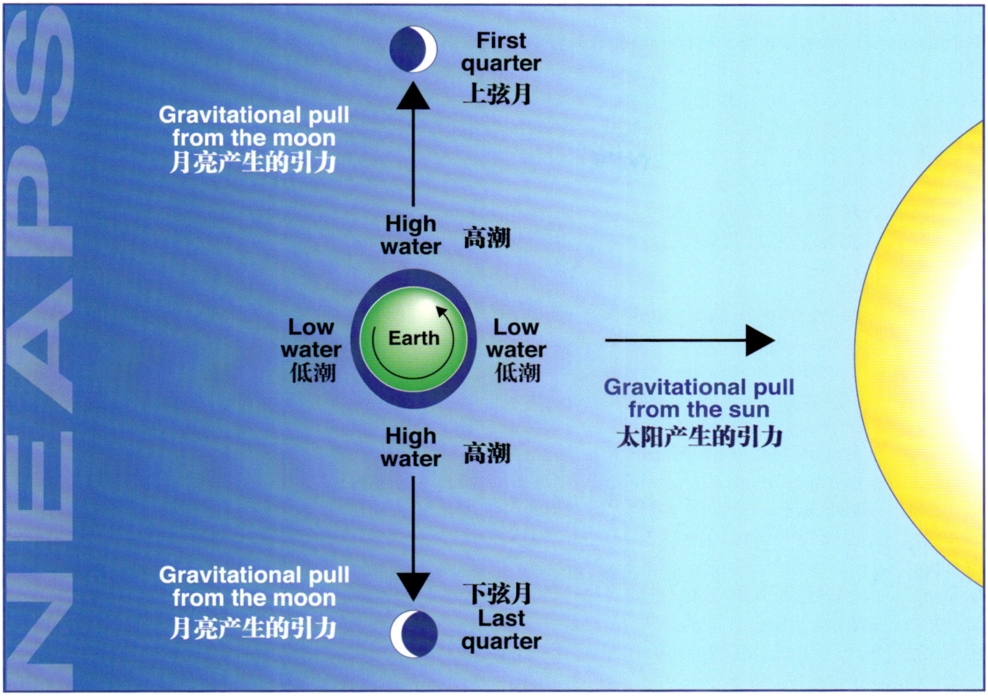

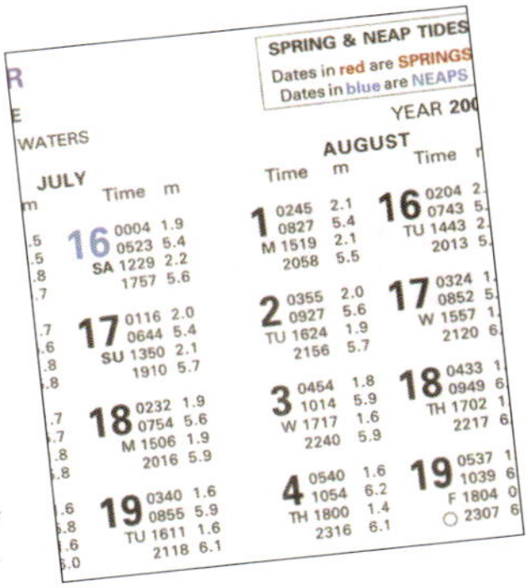

In most places high tide follows low tide on a roughly six hour cycle (i.e. two highs and two lows per day) and springs and neaps alternate on a seven day cycle.
在大多数地方，低潮后大概6小时高潮，周期往复（也就是说一天两次高潮两次低潮），大潮和小潮交替7天一个周期。

Tidal information is available from a variety of sources—a nautical almanac, local tide tables or even the Internet. Usually the times and heights of high and low water for the chosen port are given, sometimes there is also a tidal graph which gives more precise calculations.
从多种渠道都可获取潮汐信息：航海年鉴、地区潮汐表，甚至因特网。一般来说，这些渠道都给出了指定港口高低潮的水位高度和时间，有些则给出潮汐曲线图，这是更为精确的计算数据。

Tidal Streams 潮汐流

Tidal streams are the movement of water as the tide floods and ebbs and as with springs we have a greater range of water (high tide higher and low tide lower) than with neaps it follows that the tide will flood and ebb faster at springs than neaps. This information is shown on charts (as tidal diamonds) and in tidal atlases and almanacs—usually both rate of flow and direction are shown. Knowing the rate and direction allows you to make a more informed decision for example:
A passage with the tide—will be faster and use less fuel

A passage with wind against tide—could be rougher
A passage with wind and tide together—may be smoother
潮流是随着潮涌潮退带来的水流，大潮时移动的水量更大（高潮位更高，低潮位更低），小潮时水量更小，于是大潮流速更快，小潮流速更慢。海图上的潮汐方形图，以及潮汐图和航海图鉴都给出了这种信息——一般都会给出流速和方向。知道流速和流向可以帮你做出更为准确的决定。比如：
顺流航行：更快和更省油；
逆风和逆流航行：可能更颠簸；
顺风和顺流航行：可能更舒适。

Compass 罗经

To navigate at sea boaters use a compass, which allows you to steer on a particular heading, take bearings of known objects to plot your position and monitor the bearing to assess the risk of collision with other craft. Compass's point to Magnetic North. This is different from the chart which is aligned with True North. The difference between True and Magnetic North is called variation. If we are transferring bearings from a chart to use on a compass, they need to be converted from True to Magnetic. Likewise, when reading bearings from a compass they need converting to True before plotting on a chart. Variation can vary greatly between different boating areas, and changes over time. It is calculated and recorded on charts. Whilst afloat if we need to find our position and mark it on the chart, we can do this by using a 3 point fix. This allows a position on the sea to be plotted onto a chart with reference to nearby land objects.

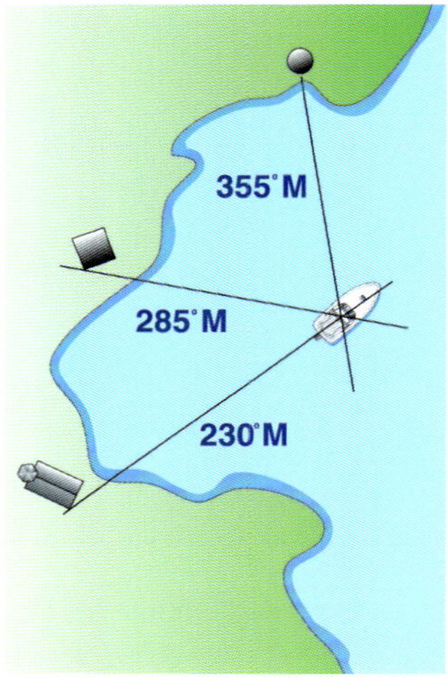

船上的人在大海上航行需要使用罗经，罗经能够帮助你往指定航向上行驶，测量已知参考物的方位角可为你确定位置，持续监测方位角还可判断碰撞风险。罗经指向磁北极。这跟以真北（地轴北极为正北）为参考系的海图不一样。真北和磁北的差叫作磁偏角。如果把图上的方位角转换成罗经方位角的时候，我们需要进行真北和磁北间的换算。比如说，从罗经上读取到一个方位角，我们需要换算成真北系统的方位角度，然后才可以画在海图上。不同地方、不同时间，磁偏角都不一样。这些在海图上都印有经计算的数据。在海上我们可以通过三点定位法画出我们的位置。也就是利用参照附近陆地的（至少三个）标定物体找到位置并画在海图上。

Electronic Navigation 电子导航

The Global Positioning System (GPS) has now become the primary navigation system for small powerboats where space for chartwork is limited.
When used in conjunction with a chart it makes progress along a pre-planned route easier. GPS systems show your current position and can also be programmed with waypoints (a position expressed in Latitude and Longitude). By entering a route using waypoints the GPS can show the

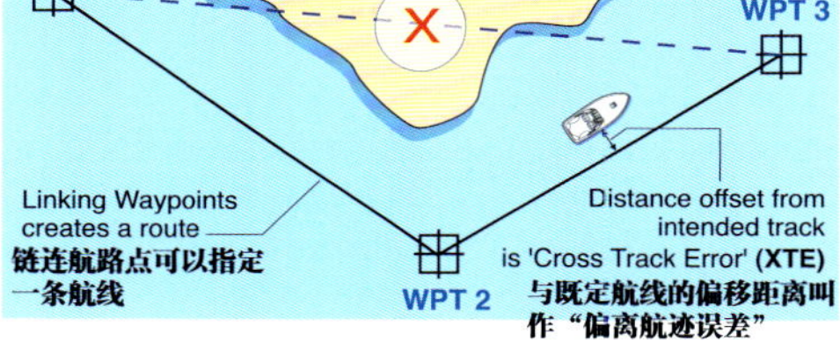

bearing and distance from one waypoint to another.
全球卫星定位系统（GPS）在今天已经变成最为重要的导航系统，其对于没有空间进行海图作业的小型机动艇尤为有用。其与海图结合使用可以使预制航线计划更为简单快速。GPS系统给出你当前的位置而且还会给出标定航路点（用经纬度表示的位置）。利用航路点输入航线，GPS可以给出一个航路点到另一个航路点的方位角和距离。

GPS can also give your speed over the ground (SOG), course over the ground (COG) and show you how far you have strayed from your intended route (cross track error - XTE).
GPS还能提供对地速度（SOG）、对地航线（COG），以及与你期望航线的偏离距离（偏离航迹误差-XTE）。

Buoyage 航标

In IALA A (as shown below) we leave the starboard cone to our starboard side when entering harbour—our boat's port and starboard side match the buoyage. In IALA B the reverse is true.
国际航道标志协会A标准中，当我们进港的时候右舷经过锥形右舷标，左右舷对应左右舷标。在国际航道标志协会B标准中，定义相反。

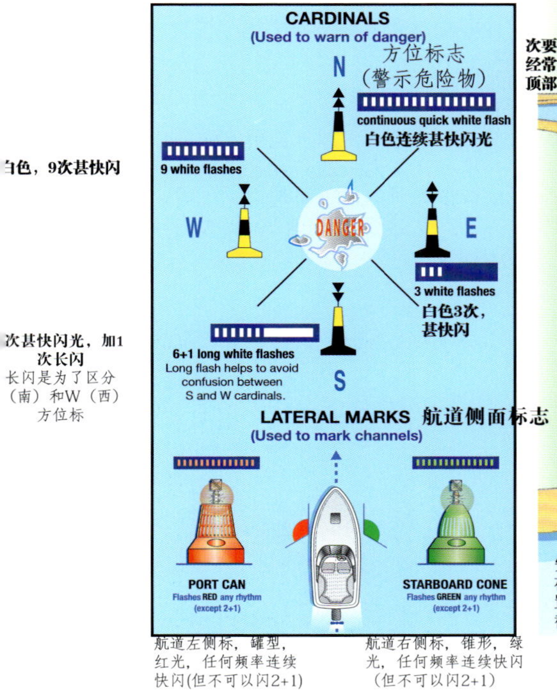

Passage Planning and Pilotage
航线计划和引航

简单的引航计划
Simple Pilotage Plan

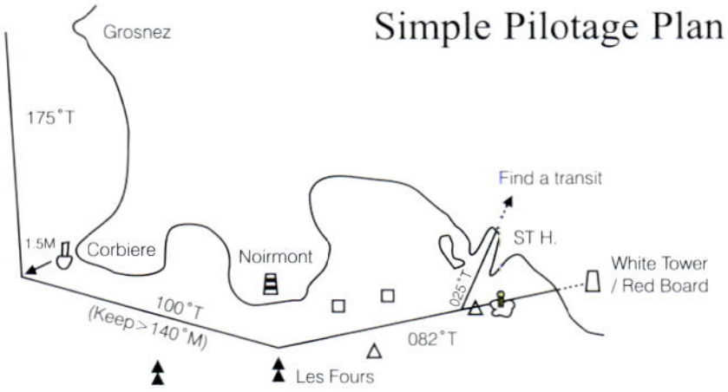

Passage planning is the ability to prepare a plan that allows you to safely navigate between two points. It will take into account: weather, stream, tidal rates, route, vessel and the experience of the crew. At the end of a passage you will use pilotage, which is the use of landmarks, buoyage, transits and water depth for departure and arrival at a known or unknown harbour or marina.
航线计划是指制订一份能帮助你安全地在两个点之间航行的计划。需要考虑流、天气、潮汐周期、航线、船只和船员的经验。在航程结束前，你需要引航技术，即利用陆上的航标、浮标、叠标，以及出发和抵达时在熟悉或不熟悉的港口或码头的水深。

Weather 天气

Weather information is available from television, radio, VHF, the Internet and your local harbour or marina. A basic understanding of wind strength, direction and what effect it has while you are out on the water is essential for the skipper of a small boat. Remember wind against the stream will make the sea state worse. (RYA Publication G133 Weather Handbook)
可以通过电视、广播、甚高频无线电、网络，以及当地港口或码头获取天气信息。了解风力、风向和对出海可能产生的影响是船长必须具备的能力。注意风顶流会使海况变差。（详见RYA出版物G133《天气预报手册》）

The Beaufort Scale and interpreting weather forecasts

蒲福风级和天气预报的解读

Force 风力	Wind speed 风速	Description 描述	Wave height 浪高	Sea state 海况	What's it like? 适合玩船吗?
0	< 1 knot < 1 节	Calm 平静无风	0 m 0米	Mirror-like 海面光滑如镜	Ideal powerboating weather 理想的机动艇出海天气
1	1–3 knots 1～3 节	Light air 软风	Up to 0.1m 不超过0.1m	Ripples on the surface 表面波纹	
2	4–6 knots 4～6 节	Light breeze 轻风	Up to 0.3m 不超过0.3m	Small wavelets with smooth crests 波峰平缓光滑	
3	7–10 knots 7～10 节	Gentle breeze 微风	Up to 0.9m 不超过0.9m	Large wavelets with crests starting to break 小波，波峰开始破裂	
4	11–16 knots 11～16 节	Moderate breeze 和风	Up to 1.5m 不超过1.5m	Large waves begin to form with white foam crests 大波，开始形成白色泡沫状波峰	Getting interesting 开始有些危险了
5	17–21 knots 17～21 节	Fresh breeze 清风	Up to 2.5m 不超过2.5m	Moderate waves and many white horses 中浪并形成很多白色浪花	Only for the more experienced 只适合更有经验者
6>	21 knots > 21 节	Strong breeze + 强风	2.5m + 2.5m及以上	Large waves + 大浪	Do something else! 玩些别的吧!

Towing 拖拽

When towing always make sure that the tow vessel is suitable in size for the task. Consider how far you will need to tow, ensure you have the correct lines and agree any charges before you start.
拖带时首先一定要确认拖引船的大小是否适合。考虑拖带的距离，确保你有合适长度的拖带缆，并且在拖带前确认支付给各方的有关费用。

Astern Tow 拖头式拖带

An astern tow is usually the easiest tow for any distance. Agree a simple communications method before you start, use a long line which will act as a shock absorber, lead the tow line through any fairleads and spread the load on both craft over the strong points. It will be much easier to steer if the tow is from ahead of the outboard or rudder and on the centre line of the craft. Outboard powered craft can use a bridle for light tows. Adjust the tow length so that if there is any sea running you aim to use a line of twice the wavelength, to ensure that the vessel under tow sits comfortably on the waves coming behind you.
拖头式拖带对任何距离的拖带来说往往都是最简单的拖航方式。拖带开始前应进行简单的沟通。使用一根足够长的缆绳，其能起到缓冲作用。把拖缆穿过导缆孔，将受力分担到适合拖带的结构强点上。拖带点在舷外机或舵前方中线的位置比较容易掌舵。对于舷外机或舷外驱动船，如果拖带载荷不大，可以配三角绳。调整拖缆长度，大概两倍波长，这样在顶浪行驶的时候，后面被拖的船也能比较舒适。

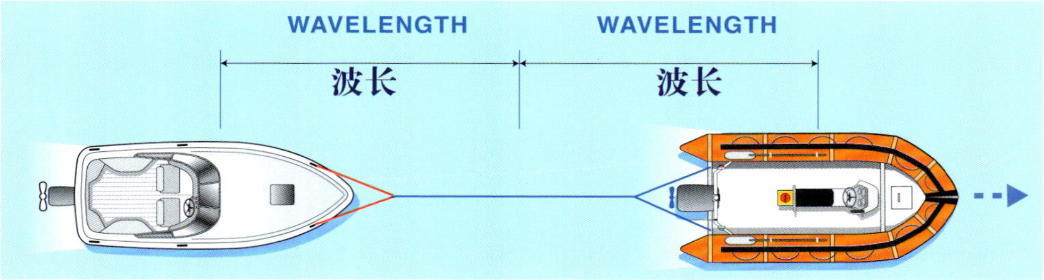

Towing Alongside 侧拷式拖带

This is more like pushing the boat. Especially good when greater control is required - in harbour, or into a berth. The tow vessels must be toed-in slightly. The rudder or outboard of the towing vessel must be behind the towed vessel. Use the bow line to keep the vessels toed-in. The stern line holds it together when you turn corners. A tug's fore spring will take nearly all the weight when moving ahead. The tug's stern spring will take nearly all the weight when moving astern.
这更像是推船，当需要较高控制能力时，比如在港口内或靠泊作业时使用。拖轮要船头稍向内。拖轮的舵或舷外机必须在被拖船后。使用艏缆保持拖轮船头向内的姿态。艉缆连接两船用于转弯。前进的时候主要通过艏倒缆受力，倒车时则通过艉倒缆传输载荷。

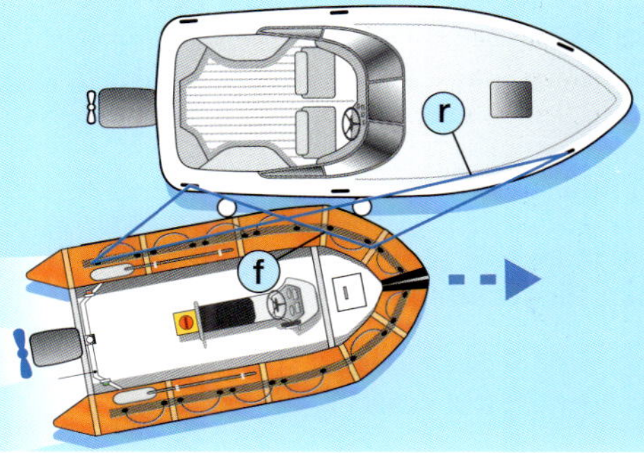

- Towing vessel 'angled in'.
  拖轮船头角度向内。
- Towing vessel well astern.
  拖轮艉在拖船尾后面。
- Spring 'f' takes load in forward. Spring 'r' in astern.
  正车时主要通过艏倒缆受力，倒车时通过艉倒缆传输载荷。

Glossary of Terms 术语汇编

蒲福风级 —— 风速的级别
Beaufort Scale —— Scale of wind speeds

助浮衣 —— 与救生衣类似，但是效果较弱
Buoyancy aid —— Similar to lifejacket, but less effective

方位标 —— 罗经定位系统，用于标注安全水域的航标
Cardinals —— Compass orientated system for buoyage marking safe water

惯性行驶 —— 空挡下船只继续前进或倒退
Carrying away —— Forward or reverse movement of craft whilst in neutral

大教堂型船身 —— W形船身
Cathedral hull —— W shaped hull

羊角 —— 用于固定缆绳的甲板装置
Cleat —— Deck fitting for securing ropes

锥形号型 —— 用于日间指示船只类型的一种号型
Cone —— Day shape identifying vessel type

D环 —— 用于把船固定在拖车上的甲板装置
D-ring —— Deck fitting for securing craft to trailer

菱形号型 —— 用于日间指示船只类型的一种号型
Diamond —— Day shape identifying vessel type

排水型船体 —— 不可滑行的船体
Displacement hull —— Non-planning hull

多利船体（平底船） —— 小型的，船底非常平的一种船体
Dory hull —— Fairly flat-bottomed hull

干式保暖服 —— 比湿式保暖服提供更多保护的防水服装
Dry suit —— Waterproof gear with more protection than wet suit

倒缆孔 —— 用于倒缆的甲板装置
Fairlead —— Deck fitting for guiding ropes

干舷 —— 船体高出水面部分的垂直高度
Freeboard —— Vertical amount of hull above water

全球卫星定位系统 —— 卫星导航系统
GPS —— Global Positioning System – satellite navigation system

让路船 —— 需要给直航船让路的船只
Give way vessel —— Vessel obliged to keep clear of stand on vessel

IALA——国际航道标志协会
IALA International Association of Marine Aids to Navigation and Lighthouse Authorities

喷射式推进器——使用高压水喷射推进和操舵的系统
Jet drive Propulsion and steering system using high pressure water

保险绳——在紧急情况下关闭发动机的绳索
Kill cord Safety lanyard that cuts out engine in an emergency

侧面航标——指示航道的航标系统
Lateral marks Identification system for buoyage marking channels

下风面——风吹向的方向或那一侧
Leeward Downwind direction/side

海上移动通信识别码——使用VHF DSC广播系统的一种船舶唯一识别编号
MMSI Unique craft identification number used with VHF DSC radio

落水人员——落水人员
MOB Man overboard

动量——船只在空挡时前进或后退（船在运动中与质量和速度有关的量，表示运动中的作用效果。与空挡无关。——译者注）
Momentum Forward or reverse movement of craft whilst in neutral

舷外机器——和舷外机的推进及操舵方式类似，但是发动机安置在船体内，推进器在船外
Outdrive Propulsion and steering system similar to outboard, but built into craft

艏缆——系在船上艏部的用于系泊的缆绳
Painter Mooring line attached to the boat

转向点——假想中的点，拐弯时船体以该点为中心做转向运动
Pivot point Imaginary point around which the hull pivots when turning

滑行船体——所配动力可以在高速时令船体离开水面滑行的船体类型
Planing hull Hull type where its power allows it to rise on top of water at speed

绘图尺——绘制导航图的仪器
Plotter Instrument used with navigation charts

螺旋桨侧推效应——螺旋桨转动产生横向侧推效果
Prop effect Transverse thrust of propeller

硬壳充气船——硬壳充气船
RIB　Rigid Inflatable Boat

尺度——锚绳和锚链的长度
Scope　Length of anchor chain and rope

半排水型船体——部分排水型、部分V形的船体
Semi-displacement hull　Part displacement, part Vee hull

轴驱推进——舷内发动机通过轴驱传输动力给螺旋桨的推进系统
Shaft drive　Propulsion system using an inboard engine

倒缆——防止船前后移动的缆绳
Spring　Mooring line restricting movement of craft fore and aft

直航船——必须保持直行的船只
Stand on vessel　Vessel obliged to hold course and speed

后驱动——参见舷外机
Stern drive　See Outdrive

水流——水流的影响
Stream　Effect of water movement

变量——正北和磁极北的差别
Variation　Difference between True and Magnetic North

V形船体——船体的描述
Vee hull　Description of hull shape

绞船索——缆绳，例如锚索
Warp　Rope, e.g. anchor warp

航路点——航程内导航用的点
Waypoint　Navigational position along route

风阻——因船体和船上部分而产生的风阻
Windage　Amount of wind resistance offered by hull and superstructure

XTE——偏离航线距离——航行时偏离预定航迹的距离
XTE　Cross Track Error—distance offset from intended track when navigating

WHY JOIN THE RYA?

OVER 80

RYA member reward partners

Influencing policy on over 250 marine protected areas in UK waters

Fighting for members' rights on more than 20 Current Affairs topics

OnBoard has introduced over

800,000

children to sailing

60,000+

disabled people have been able to experience sailing through the RYA Sailability programme

Membership costs from only

12p per day

2,500 international training centres including the UK, Australia, New Zealand, South Africa, Indonesia, Thailand and the USA

250,000

course completions each year

OVER 815,000

visits to our Knowledge and Advice web pages a year